> Col. Giammona,
> It was an honor to meet you. Thank you for raising the standard!
> Josh K
> Philippians 3:14

THE STANDARD

Discovering Jesus as the
Standard for Masculinity

JOSH KHACHADOURIAN

© 2020 by Josh Khachadourian - www.standard59.com

Printed in the United States of America

Cover design and artwork by Justin Stewart - www.justifii.com.

All rights reserved. No part of this publication may be reproduced, stored in a retrieval system, or transmitted in any form or by any means without the prior written permission of the author/publisher. The exception is brief quotations.

ISBN 978-1-7345493-0-0

Scripture Quotations

Unless otherwise indicated, all Scripture quotations are taken from NEW AMERICAN STANDARD BIBLE®, Copyright © 1960,1962,1963,1968, 1971,1972,1973,1975,1977,1995 by The Lockman Foundation. Used by permission."

Scripture quotations labeled TPT are from The Passion Translation®. Copyright © 2017, 2018 by Passion & Fire Ministries, Inc. Used by permission. All rights reserved. ThePassionTranslation.com.

Scripture Quotations labeled NET are from the New English Translation NET Bible® copyright ©1996-2017 All rights reserved. Build 30170414 by Biblical Studies Press, L.L.C.

Scripture quotations labeled MSG are taken from THE MESSAGE, copyright © 1993, 2002, 2018 by Eugene H. Peterson. Used by permission of NavPress. All rights reserved. Represented by Tyndale House Publishers, Inc.

Scripture Quotations labeled NKJV are taken from the New King James Version®. Copyright © 1982 by Thomas Nelson. Used by permission. All rights reserved.

Scripture Quotations labeled Wuest Translation are from The New Testament, an expanded translation by Kenneth S. Wuest. Copyright Wm. B. Eerdmans Publishing Co. 1961. All rights reserved.

FREE DOWNLOAD

12 STRATEGIES EVERY MAN NEEDS TO BE POWERED BY PURPOSE

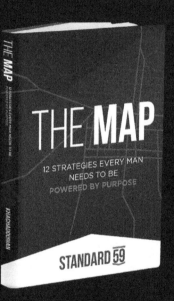

There are Rules to the Game Every Man Must Honor.

Inside the MAP you will Get Access to 12 Strategies YOU must Implement and Execute to Smash Unbelief, Take Your Territory and Expand The Kingdom.

RAISE YOUR STANDARD AND DOWNLOAD YOUR MAP NOW

https://www.standard59.com/THEMAP

BE THE MAN YOU ARE CREATED TO BE!

Listen to the Raising The Standard Podcast to Get Weekly Motivation for the Kingdom Driven Man

LEADERSHIP, MINDSET AND DEVELOPMENT FOR THE KINGDOM MAN

Listen Today on Your Favorite Podcast Platform

CONTENTS

Book I | Self - Mastery
THE **MEASURING REED**

- 23. SELF-MASTERY
- 29. JESUS IS A MAN OF DISCIPLINE
- 35. JESUS IS DILIGENT
- 41. JESUS DEMONSTRATES RESTRAINT
- 47. JESUS HAS A PLAN
- 55. JESUS IS CONFIDENT IN HIS IDENTITY
- 65. JESUS WON'T BE CONFINED TO MAN'S DEFINITION
- 71. JESUS IS A MAN OF PRAYER
- 77. JESUS VALUES BEING ALONE
- 81. JESUS DOES NOT COMPROMISE

Book II | Leadership
THE **SHEPHERDS STAFF**

- 89. LEADERSHIP
- 93. JESUS IS A SERVANT LEADER
- 99. JESUS IS A TEACHER
- 105. JESUS IS A COACH
- 111. JESUS INVITES US INTO EXPERIENCE
- 117. JESUS RESPONDS TO QUESTIONS WITH QUESTIONS
- 123. JESUS IS AN ORGANIZATIONAL LEADER
- 129. JESUS PRIORITIZES REST
- 135. JESUS THE BUSINESSMAN
- 143. JESUS REVEALS THE FATHER

Book III | Communication
THE **CHISEL**

- 151. JESUS IS THE MASTER COMMUNICATOR
- 155. JESUS THE STORYTELLER
- 161. JESUS HAS A SENSE OF HUMOR
- 167. JESUS SPEAKS IN MYSTERIES THAT INVITE DISCOVERY
- 173. JESUS IS A FRIEND
- 177. JESUS IS A MENTOR
- 181. JESUS HAS AN INNER CIRCLE

Book IV | Empathy
THE FISHING NET

- 187. FISHER OF MEN
- 191. JESUS SHOWS EMOTION
- 195. JESUS MODELS ALL THE FRUIT OF THE SPIRIT
- 203. JESUS LIBERATES WOMEN
- 209. JESUS IS GENTLE
- 213. JESUS MODELS HUMILITY
- 217. JESUS IS A MAN OF COMPASSION
- 221. JESUS DEFENDS THE WEAK
- 225. JESUS FORGIVES AND RESTORES

Book V | Confrontation
THE SWORD

- 231. THE SWORD
- 235. JESUS IS A MAN OF TRUTH
- 239. JESUS IS A MAN OF COURAGE
- 245. JESUS IS A MAN OF ENDURANCE
- 251. JESUS IS A MAN OF CONFRONTATION
- 255. JESUS PROVIDES CORRECTION
- 261. JESUS IS DISCERNING OF MAN
- 267. JESUS IS NOT SAFE
- 271. JESUS IS A MAN OF PURPOSE AND PASSION

Book VI | LOVE
THE CROSS

- 277. THE WORK OF THE CROSS
- 279. THE WAY OF THE CROSS
- 281. THE CALL

INTRODUCTION

THE #1 FEAR MEN HAVE IS BEING A FAILURE…

There is a deep need in the heart of every man to achieve greatness, overcome challenges and pursue excellence. At the core of our beings we are hard-wired to overcome obstacles, compete and win. We want to 'have it all.' In our quest to discover our life's meaning we pick up shallow pursuits, get side tracked constantly and find it easy to lose our course as we map out our goals and pursue our ambitions. Underneath all of our busy activity is our need to upgrade every area of our life, a desire to play bigger and take our game to the next level.

Many men today are searching for meaning. Our search to have it all is connected with our search for significance. Never before has there been a time where we have so much information available to us through our present-day media machine. Right now endless shelves of books, internet articles, blogs and podcasts are waiting to be downloaded. We have no shortage of opinions and theories on the topic of masculinity and what true manhood is.

The down side to such readily-available media is that everyone has a platform…whether they speak truth or not. It can be overwhelming and confusing as to who has the corner on what true masculinity is and how manhood should be defined. So many voices have emerged to lead, shape and show men 'the way,' which has only exasperated the current crisis going on with men. It's no wonder many are confused. There is no question masculinity is under attack. We face a real crisis and real men need to emerge.

In my quest to have it all, I paid a high price in my investment of time and dollars. My quest led me to years of training. I read countless books, consumed endless hours of media, took courses, and worked with coaches, only to discover that the man I was aspiring to be was found in a book written thousands of years ago. I am talking about the ancient wisdom contained within the Bible.

In my journey to become the man I always wanted to be, I discovered an often-overlooked model Jesus provides men. I found a pattern in His life through what He models, His methods and His actions. He is the standard by which you and I are called to live up to, and once you see this everything changes.

JESUS IS THE STANDARD.

THERE IS A CRISIS AMONG MEN

There is a debate raging over masculinity. Influencers, movements and corporations are fighting to define what it means for you to be a man. With definitions like 'toxic masculinity' invading the conversation, there is a tug of war over defining what the standards are for men. If you feel like your identity as a man is constantly in the crosshairs, make no mistake…it is, and it's not your fault.

Today's man is suffering from:

- Fatherlessness
- Lack of purpose
- Lack of identity
- Lack of vision

We have lost the definition of manhood; men are searching for their sense of value and meaning. Today's man is chasing status because he lost his significance, he does not know his authority and does not respect himself. The results of this is leaving men in a lethargic state, complacent and bored, meandering through mediocrity and it's carrying a devastating impact on our families and our society.

In 2018, news reporter Tucker Carlson did a 4-part special on FOX called "Men in America" where he discussed the shocking statistics among men. I have outlined a few here from his report.

- The average American man will die 5 years before the average American woman
- Men are more than 2x's as likely than women to become alcoholics and die of a drug overdose
- 77% of all suicides in America are men and the overall rate is increasing at a dramatic pace, 43% increase from 1997 to 2014
- Over 90% of inmates are male
- Men lag behind in graduation rates from high school and college

- Boys have more discipline problems
- 1 in 5 high school boys are diagnosed for hyperactivity, many are medicated
- Men are the larger consumers of pain medication
- Fewer get married and stay married, 1 in 5 American children live only with their mothers, this is 2x the rate since 1970
- 70% of men are either overweight or obese
- Almost all mass shooters are men

"American men are failing in body, in mind and spirit…this is a crisis"
- Tucker Carlson

https://youtu.be/LrhHkQhglig

As the media attempts to shape our view of men from how we are portrayed in sitcoms and movies to what the news anchors, talk show and radio hosts are saying, the banner of political correctness is flaunted to silence the man's voice in attempt to force us into a box, resulting in:

1. Men becoming ashamed of who we really are and how to express our God given identity.

2. Men feeling threatened to break out into our true identity for fear of consequences.

Today's modern man is at the cross-roads of an identity crisis. Double minded and undecided on how to navigate through these seemingly perilous waters, he is left standing there, staring at the limited options in front of him. Feeling lethargic and lacking energy, going through the motions as husband, getting by at work with no passion and sense of purpose and checked out as father.

The masculinity spectrum in our present-day culture hosts the entire range of the mask's men wear from the bravado of the seemingly alpha male flexing hard to demonstrate an image of the self-made man flashing his trophies of materialism, all the way to the submissive and subservient beta male afraid to offend anyone and willing to appease all.

What is the modern-day Christian Man to do?
Who is he to be?
Where are our role models and how did we get here?

This book is intended for the modern Christian man. Before we reframe manhood and present our model for how God created us to rule in the earth and demonstrate His Kingdom in today's fallen world, we must first examine how we arrived at this point.

CHRISTIANITY HAS BEEN FEMINIZED

There are multiple layers to how men have begun to view Christianity through a skewed lens where the Christian faith is associated with more feminine qualities and characteristics. In the late 1700's as America was entering into the Industrial Revolution men were leaving their farm work and for the first time leaving their homes and families to enter into the workforce. With men out of the home and in the factories, women began to take the lead teaching what were considered 'spiritual qualities.' With women making up almost 75% of the congregations at this time, the church programs began to shift to center on women. The church services were focused on catering to females as their pre-dominant audience and in turn started driving male attendance down even more.

This entire process listed below further drove men away from Christianity.

- Men being absent from the home for the day
- Women assuming spiritual leadership in the home
- High attendance of women in American congregations
- Increased focus on feminine centered programs in churches

This in turn created a cycle where the men that were drawn to church leadership often lacked the masculine qualities that their peers who entered other professions traditionally displayed. As a result, women in the church dominated as Sunday school teachers and leaders within the church (under the leadership of a less than masculine man). This had a profound impact on the boys as they will now associate Christianity and church leadership with femininity (feminine qualities).

The Church in America starting in the 1800's was largely made up of women. With very few men choosing to go to theology school. This created a vacuum of men as role models for young boys within the church. This gap has shaped multiple generations, their view of Christianity and the way they see and relate to Jesus.

WHERE ARE OUR FATHERS?

Physically Absent

To compound the issue of the absence of men in the church and serving as teachers, leaders and role models, we are suffering from the absence of fathers. This manifests in a variety of scenarios. With divorce rates skyrocketing many men are absent from their children, some have shared rights and limited access to make an impact, teach and train their children. While a proportion of men turn their back on their families and go down the road of the deadbeat dad. According to the 2017 U.S. Census Bureau, 19.7 million children, more than 1 in 4, live without a father in the home.

Emotionally Absent

There is a plague upon us of fathers that are physically present in the home but emotionally unavailable. These are the guys that don't know how to truly connect with their children because they are either missing the tools and don't know how to foster connection or they willingly check out emotionally leaving the heavy lifting of parenting to their wives. They are pre-occupied with work, the game and even when they are in the same room with their kids they are not present or intentional. They sit there like a zombie scrolling through their phone or zoning out watching tv. This is the lazy uninterested and unintentional approach to parenting.

Spiritually Absent

The last category I want to hit are the spiritually absentee fathers, at home and in the church. Now obviously the emotionally checked out by default will almost always fall into this category, however there is another segment of good fathers that are intentional with their parenting but are failing as the spiritual leader in the house. Similar to what we observed happen throughout history with men leaving the spiritual influence to the women we are still seeing this play out today. Generations of men have passed where there was no spiritual fathering and leadership exhibited, in turn massive amounts of men have never had spiritual role models and have become spiritual absentee fathers. This impacts boys as they are developing their thoughts towards Christianity and forming their perspective on what a real man is and relating to God as their father. With no models for biblical manhood our young men have sought their definition of manhood from modern day culture.

JESUS IS THE MODEL FOR MASCULINITY

Jesus is our model for masculinity and this view has been largely absent and untaught. The church rightly emphasizes presenting Jesus as the Son of God, who died for our sins, and defeated death. Jesus is the King of Kings, He is the Lord of Lords and the Son of God, however His favorite self-descriptor was 'Son of Man.' Jesus is referred to as 'Son of Man' over 80 times within the four gospels of Matthew, Mark, Luke and John. This title identifies Him in His humanity, Jesus is most comfortable relating to those He teaches and ministers to from His humanity. The Bible tells us that Jesus willingly emptied Himself and chose to self-limit His power by becoming a man.

> "…who, although He existed in the form of God, did not regard equality with God a thing to be grasped, but emptied Himself, taking the form of a bond-servant, and being made in the likeness of men."
>
> Philippians 2:6-7

The theological doctrine for Jesus existing as 100% God and 100% man at the same time is known as 'kenosis' and signifies His emptying and self-imposed limitation of power. Jesus lived His existence on earth having a divine and human nature at the same time. The reason He refers to Himself as 'Son of Man' is because the 'first man' Adam failed when he disobeyed God. Jesus appears as what the bible calls the 'second man' to redeem everything that was lost when Adam sinned (1 Corinthians 15:45-47).

THE MISSING LINK

In our understanding of Jesus as Lord many have overlooked His role as man and entrance into humanity in the fulfillment of His mission to offer us salvation. Sadly, many men feel unworthy to draw close to Jesus and instead view Him as a distant, out of reach Lord that we can never relate to, we perceive Him as detached from our daily struggles. We have lost sight of Jesus in His humanity. We may revere Him as Lord but we miss what He accomplished, modeled and exemplified for us as man by taking on human flesh.

I would like to take you on a journey of exploring not only the words and message of Jesus, but His actions, His methods and what He modeled.

I advise you to put aside the image of Jesus you may have fashioned to fit your belief system; the image of Jesus you inherited from your well-intentioned (yet inaccurate) religious traditions.

- Throw out that feminine, wispy healer who prances through the pages of your Sunday school book.
- The stoic, emotionless and distant stained-glass character who is unrelatable.
- The social justice warrior, consumed with a fantasy doctrine of fairness.
- The one-sided portrayal of the Son of Man that has been twisted and manipulated to serve a political and religious purpose.

See Him in his humanity, His form is shaped by His work, His hands are calloused from handling building materials and tools for the majority of His earthly life. He sweats in the heat of the day.

His feet are covered in dirt from the paths and backroads He travels as He makes his way from town to town. He is not a pristine European picture of a sad, depressed sorry excuse for a man. He is fierce, He is dangerous and He is not safe.

Come Meet the Man Christ Jesus…and Forever Be Changed.

I warn you…Jesus does not easily fit into our nice boxes and pre-supposed attitudes.
He is not only a Lamb; He is a roaring Lion.
He is not safe. He is offensive.
He will offend your religious beliefs and political mindsets.
He carries a sword.
And He will cut you to the bone, dividing your soul from your spirit man.
He will reveal your innermost thoughts and intent.
All of this for the purpose of changing you into who He created and called you to be.

THE BOXES

THE CHALLENGES OF PRESENT-DAY MANHOOD

As men, we are faced with various pressures every day. This is not new; this has been going on since we were young.

As boys rough housing and during our interactions with friends and siblings, we are taught there are different ways you act in different situations and locations. Be controlled in the house, go outside if you want to be wild, be quiet when you are in church, pay attention at school, be aggressive on the field.

These are the boxes we are introduced to as we are raised by our parents, instructed by our teachers and professors and observe society's ways. We learn this lesson very clearly: we must fit in the box.

The box looks like go to school, graduate from college, get a 'good' job, be a 'good' Christian, contributing member of society, raise a family, etc.

It really doesn't matter if the above statement is your exact experience or not. We all have boxes that we have been trained and conformed to fit into, whether that example represents your box well or not.

These boxes are enforced through every stage of life.

Think of school students who play competitive sports. Within the school walls, they are taught to act a certain way, be a good student (even be an over-achiever), demonstrate kindness, treat everyone with respect, and be humble. That same student on the field is taught to be aggressive, and sideline parents and coaches even scream at them to play harder, don't miss the shot, make the tackle, kick the goal…

As we mature through life's stages, the scenes change and we are forced into different boxes as we walk out our life. Although the sidelines have become empty, in our minds, voices still echo to push harder and avoid failure.

For those who are climbing the corporate ladder, we must learn to be high performers, exhibit drive and constantly watch our back, keep up our image, and be skilled at workplace politics, knowing where our advocates are and discerning our opponents.

As entrepreneurs, we battle the stress of maintaining the bottom line, employee engagement, balancing the books, somehow not taking all our work home with us at night, and defending from competition…and of course closing the next deal to keep putting bread on our tables.

As manual laborers and employees, we put in a hard day's work, get up early, work hard to provide, balance our bills, pay down debt, and maintain savings to provide our families the best we can offer.

As husbands, we need to act a certain way. It is not always healthy to bring the energy and emotion from our work into the house. We need to be dedicated husbands, attentive and engaged, present and intentional.

As fathers, we need to play the part of instructor, healer, coach and leader. It's a crucial balance of compassion and discipline. We carry the responsibility of raising the next generation with honor, ethics and integrity. The boxes represent our various roles through our stations in life, and they are not inherently bad. It's crucial to be engaged at work, committed to our wives and dedicated to our children.

Some of us are good at balancing, but most are not. We need to show up differently in each of these areas, gracefully making transitions from one box to the next. Sometimes we also need to break the boxes and limitations that are placed on us as we transition to and from each area of our life. Jesus came so that we could live the abundant life. What does the abundant life look like for us today? Is it some spiritual state of mind that we are ever reaching for, but never quite attaining?

Jesus is our ultimate model for abundant living. He came to model what we can have, attain and be, and He certainly could not be conformed to any boxes society and His culture tried to contain Him in. He is the ultimate box breaker.

He moves gracefully and with precision through life's situations. Like us, He plays many roles, has multiple titles and serves many people in different ways.

What you will find in the pages that follow is a blueprint that Jesus left us. He did not come to give us a rule book or three-step formulas.

> He came to give us life; He is Life.
> He came to give us truth; He is Truth.
> He came to show us the way; He is the Way.
> He is the blueprint.

Choosing to follow Jesus is not formulaic living. It's not a WWJD (what would Jesus do?) bracelet and trying our hardest by sheer will power to be the best Christian we can be. All of our feeble efforts birthed in the energy of our flesh to "try" and be good Christians will eventually fizzle out. Unsustainable, we will grow weary, get tired and all efforts that began with our natural energy will ultimately fall flat.

The invitation Jesus offers us is to be re-born. This new birth is an exchange of life, an adoption, where we are now pronounced the sons of God and live by the leading of His Holy Spirit living through us.

Examining Jesus as the model is not meant to bring us into bondage or present an out-of-reach Lord and Savior who leaves us feeling like failures, never living up to what He has called us to be. Jesus became the 'protokonos,' which is the Greek word for the prototype or 'firstborn' of what we are to become (Colossians 1:15).

The Christian life is a process of growth – It is a daily walk of being conformed into His image. It is less of me and more of Him or as John the Baptist stated:

"He must increase and I must decrease."

The apostle Paul said it this way: "Be transformed…by the renewing of your mind" (Romans 12:2). In his letter to the Ephesians, Paul writes:

> "…until we all attain (reach the goal) to the unity of the faith, and of the knowledge of the Son of God – a mature man, attaining to the measure of Christ's full stature."
>
> Ephesians 4:13

The apostle John also writes about our proper pattern of growth as we progress in our spiritual maturity levels, starting as children, progressing to young men and eventually developing into fathers (1 John 2:12-14). This is the spiritual growth pattern that all believers are meant to progress through.

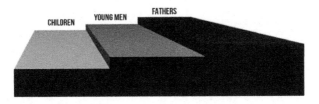

With all the roles we have as men and considering the many confusing examples in the world today, my goal is to present a fresh perspective on Jesus in His humanity: the way He acted, the model He provides and an examination and reflection on His operating principles and how we may apply them today in our lives. He is our prototype, and we are to be modeled after Him.

"FOLLOW ME"

-Jesus

This book is divided into the following six sections:

SELF-MASTERY

In Book 1 we will meet Jesus, the One who walks with a measuring reed. He is the standard by which we measure everything, and He sets the standard for us today.

LEADERSHIP

In Book 2 we will follow Him as our fearless leader. He leads and guides us with a rod in His hand. He offers us protection and provision and calls us to do the same for others.

COMMUNICATION

In Book 3 we will see and hear the way He delivers His message and how His words shape and form us. Dividing soul from spirit and revealing our thoughts and intents, His words pull us towards our purpose.

EMPATHY

In Book 4 we will see Him as the fisher of men. He captivates and captures hearts through the way He relates to us, the connection He establishes and emotion He demonstrates.

CONFRONTATION

In Book 5 we will learn that He is not a safe Savior. He deconstructs, tears down, challenges, confronts, and cuts through anything that seeks to stand in the way of others coming to the truth.

LOVE

In Book 6 we will look at His mission in physical form on earth, finished with His embrace of the cross and followed by His ascension as He invites us to live an elevated life.

HOW TO USE THIS BOOK

This is by no means an academically-thorough commentary or exhaustive study on all of the titles, works and methods of Jesus. It is, however, designed to showcase Jesus and some of the attributes He exhibited as a man; attributes we can learn from, model and apply in our daily lives and individual leadership journeys.

My hope is that you read this book in its entirety, although it will be profitable to select an attribute or section of the book for study based on your current situation or a circumstance you may be facing. Feel free to use this book as you are led and need to. Each attribute will have a teaching to read followed by a coaching section.

Content
You will learn about an aspect of Jesus with real life examples from the Bible that illustrate His behaviors and actions.

Coaching
I will serve as your coach, providing pressure, direction and suggestions as you work to apply what you learn into your everyday walk.

SCRIPTURE QUOTATIONS AND TRANSLATIONS USED

Within this book you will find numerous quotations from a variety of Bible translations and paraphrases. The original languages of the Bible are layered with depth that some Bible translations communicate better than others. In my personal Bible study time, I enjoy comparing translations and going to the original language dictionaries to uncover the deeper meanings hidden within the text.

I purposefully quote scriptures from various translations to provide the fullest picture of the context, thoughts and revelation that is being communicated.

> **NASB**
> NEW AMERICAN STANDARD BIBLE
> THE MAJORITY OF THE SCRIPTURE REFERENCES WILL BE TAKEN FROM THE NEW AMERICAN STANDARD BIBLE (NASB), UNLESS OTHERWISE NOTED, ASSUME A VERSE I INCLUDE IS FROM THE NASB.

I also pull from other translations that I have listed with their abbreviations below.

TRANSLATION GUIDE

THE PASSION TRANSLATION	TPT
NEW ENGLISH TRANSLATION	NET
THE MESSAGE BIBLE	MSG
KING JAMES VERSION	KJV
NEW KING JAMES VERSION	NKJV
WUEST TRANSLATION	WUEST

Book I | Self - Mastery

THE **MEASURING REED**

SELF-MASTERY

JESUS IS A MAN OF DISCIPLINE

JESUS IS DILIGENT

JESUS DEMONSTRATES RESTRAINT

JESUS HAS A PLAN

JESUS IS CONFIDENT IN HIS IDENTITY

JESUS WON'T BE CONFINED TO MAN'S DEFINITION

JESUS IS A MAN OF PRAYER

JESUS VALUES BEING ALONE

JESUS DOES NOT COMPROMISE

"And Jesus kept increasing in wisdom and stature, and in favor with God and men."

Luke 2:52

SELF-MASTERY

MINDSET

Recent studies in neuroscience point to developing the right way of thinking to continue to learn and develop ourselves. This commitment to personal development is referred to as a 'growth mindset.' The opposite of this 'growth mindset' has been referred to as a fixed mindset, which is not focused on change, continuous learning or the development of self. Long before the personal development industry was launched, before guru's, courses and countless books were written on the topic of becoming your best self, changing your mindset and overcoming limiting beliefs, we have had the Bible. God's Word is the foundation upon which the core teachings of many personal development programs were built. The most prominent teachers in the history of personal development have made millions of dollars from teaching people truths found in the Bible.

Before teachings on goal setting, God told the Old Testament prophet Habakkuk:

> "Then the Lord answered me and said, 'Record the vision and inscribe it on tablets, that the one who reads it may run.'"
> Habakkuk 2:2

King Solomon, the wisest and wealthiest man who ever lived, also confirms what present day neuroscience now tells us in the book of Proverbs about our thought patterns:

> "For as he thinks within himself, so he is."
> Proverbs 23:7a

The Apostle Paul writes the following instructions to the believers in the first century about the power of mindsets, instructions for prosperity in all areas and teaches us how to guard our thought life.

> "Keep thinking about things above, not things on the earth."
>
> Colossians 3:2 (NET)

> "And do not be conformed to this world, but be transformed by the renewing of your mind, so that you may prove what the will of God is, that which is good and acceptable and perfect."
>
> Romans 12:2

> "Finally, brothers and sisters, whatever is true, whatever is worthy of respect, whatever is just, whatever is pure, whatever is lovely, whatever is commendable, if something is excellent or praiseworthy, think about these things."
>
> Philippians 4:8 (NET)

> "We are destroying speculations and every lofty thing raised up against the knowledge of God, and we are taking every thought captive to the obedience of Christ."
>
> 2 Corinthians 10:5

These verses are a small sampling of powerful ideas, that when put into action can be life-changing. Countless pages of script were God-breathed to instruct and lead us into what Jesus calls the abundant life. All of the most famous teachings on developing yourself, achieving your goals and self-leadership are found in the oldest book in history: The Bible – God's Word.

Jesus carries a message that goes straight to the fixed mindsets of the day. He challenges the traditional way of thinking and viewing God, the world and each of our lives. He not only speaks in a way that attracts those who have 'growth mindsets,' but He also speaks in a way that cultivates an appetite for learning and the desire to change. In His first public message recorded in Matthew, Jesus issues a call to action to all who can hear:

> "From that time Jesus began to preach and say, 'Repent, for the kingdom of heaven is at hand.'"
>
> Matthew 4:17

The word 'repent' in the original language is the Greek word metanoeō. It is translated as 'to think differently' and 'to change one's mind for the better.'

The self-help industry has certainly borrowed many foundational truths from the Word of God and have re-purposed eternal principles as 'secrets.' They have marketed biblical teachings as new strategies for living your best life. Undoubtedly they are not new, but undeniably God has been removed. The major mistake with 'self-help' is that it has 'me' as the center of the equation.

Jesus shows us a new way of living, by the invitation He offers us. We have responsibility in this relationship, however there is a notable difference here. Most of the self-help philosophy is rooted with 'self' in the center.

- "If I can just focus all of my energy…"
- "If I can commit to my goal…"
- "If I can will myself to make it happen, it will happen."

This is the flawed message of the 'self-life.' I will do it myself, by myself and for myself. The central focus of a man following Christ is in direct opposition to the gospel of self-development apart from God. With Christ in the center, the self is removed and Jesus assumes Lordship within our life. This does not cancel our need to work hard, commit to our goals and use our natural endurance, but it does mean we have submitted our plans and are in alignment with God's will for our lives.

In our pursuit to become the man we are called to be, we want to live our life to the fullest and maximize our potential. Men must be dedicated to our mission, like a soldier enlisted in military service. The Apostle Paul instructs his spiritual son, Timothy, to train like an athlete so that he may obtain the victor's crown. This trophy is reserved for those who have lived an overcoming life (2 Tim 2:3-5).

Obtaining the victor's crown means we have lived up to our full potential, we have run our race in such a way that we maximized our impact to fulfill our purpose. As a result, we obtained our prize, which the Bible tells us is reserved only for the overcomers.

Enrollment into the school of the Spirit is a requirement. In this school, we submit to the Holy Spirit as our teacher, guide and counselor. There are many things we will learn and various teaching methods the Lord will use in our transformation.

His process is to break, and then build. This process is dynamic and will be repeated in different areas throughout our lives as we progress through different times within our life. The Bible says that Jesus learned obedience. We are not above our master and leader, so we too must learn obedience in the school of the Spirit.

> **We must master ourselves and embrace self-leadership which is rooted in being self-less**

THE MEASURING REED

Jesus is a builder; He was a builder in His natural life and He is still building today. He carries a measuring reed and builds upon a solid foundation with symmetry and structure.

Can we become more like Jesus? Here in book one, we will examine His life; to learn and model what this looks like and apply it to our daily routines. We will install new programs, rituals and habits that will empower us to live a life that overcomes.

We will discover and examine one aspect of Jesus at a time. We must master ourselves and embrace self-leadership, which is rooted in being selfless. Once we have encountered Jesus and embraced His life and strength, we can learn to employ discipline in every area of our lives to encounter true freedom.

"The soul of a lazy man desires, and has nothing; but the soul of the diligent shall be made rich."

Proverbs 13:4 (NKJV)

JESUS IS A MAN OF DISCIPLINE

The first followers of Jesus are referred to as disciples. The word 'disciple' comes from the root word 'discipline.' In general, a disciple can be compared to a learner. The root word discipline can be translated as 'a calling to soundness of mind, to moderation and self-control.' A disciple's life will be marked by self-control. The ability to forfeit immediate pleasure for a greater goal will be a hallmark of those who carry the title of disciple.

Jesus demonstrated discipline throughout His earthly life. When you look at His years on planet earth, three decades would be dedicated as a period of preparation and living out the human experience in obscurity without the title of Rabbi or Teacher. He would be a submitted child to His earthly parents and He would be a dedicated son and a committed workman long before launching His public ministry.

Once in the public eye, He would show self-restraint by not fully revealing Himself when it would clearly offer Him an earthly advantage and play to human pride and ego (but derail His mission). As the God-Man, He is cloaked in the garments of humility. On more than one occasion, He could have demonstrated a supernatural act that would utterly destroy His opposition and win the crowd. This would be opposed to His purpose.

Jesus came to earth and walked with absolute focus on His mission and calling, which was His finished work on the cross. The Bible records that before the foundations of the world the Lamb was slain, speaking of the work that Jesus would come to accomplish and fulfill. His life was a human existence of extreme discipline, a life of sacrifice and self-restraint.

> **The ability to forfeit immediate pleasure for a greater goal will be a hallmark of those who carry the title of disciple**

Jesus modeled discipline and demonstrated what it means to be a disciple through His relationship with His Father. Part of the practice of discipline is being in submission. Jesus was submitted to the will of His Father. In that agonizing scene in the garden of Gethsemane, hours before the cross, Jesus prays, "Not my will, but Yours be done." This demonstration of complete submission to the point of death was the cost of discipleship in the life of Jesus. Jesus stated to the crowd who was enamored with His words that:

> "If anyone wants to follow me, let him take up his cross, deny himself and follow me."
>
> Luke 9:23

The Passion Translation states it this way;

> "Jesus said to all of his followers, 'If you truly desire to be my disciple, you must disown your life completely, embrace my 'cross' as your own, and surrender to my ways. For if you choose self-sacrifice, giving up your lives for my glory, you will embark on a discovery of more and more of true life. But if you choose to keep your lives for yourselves, you will lose what you try to keep.'"
>
> Luke 9:23-24 (TPT)

The ultimate sign of discipline that flows from Jesus and to every follower is a life of self-denial.

The cross is central to the mission of Jesus and is likewise central in the life of anyone who chooses to follow Him. Deny yourself, pick up your cross and follow Him. Discipleship isn't free…there is a cost involved. The cost for Jesus was the cross. The cost for you will be the same.

Thankfully we are not under first century Roman rule and there are no more physical crucifixions. Although being a Christian is extremely unpopular at the moment, we are not being persecuted to the point of death in America. So, what then does it mean to pick up your cross? What does it look like to deny yourself?

The act of denying ourselves is part of what the cross looks like in our life

Jesus is our ultimate example of one who laid everything aside, an ultimate denial of all our human nature craves in order to obtain the prize. The prize for Jesus was to purchase our salvation, pay a ransom that no one else could pay to give what no one else could give: an inheritance, that we would be called the sons of God. This is what drove Jesus to accomplish the goal.

Jesus stated that a servant is not above his master. We will walk a road of discipline and self-denial on our way to becoming who He calls us to be. We employ discipline for our benefit; for what it transforms us into and what we obtain. Being a strong spiritual man is about the process of growth, development and maturity. There is a prize to be obtained, but it is who we become through the process of transformation that is most powerful and extremely rewarding. Every athlete disciplines their body so they may obtain the prize. In the process, they are changed. This is how it is when you decide to follow Jesus and become a disciple.

THE DECISION PRECEDES THE DISCIPLINE

The willingness and self-regulation to deny what may be pleasurable in order to obtain the prize later is what the Apostle Paul lived out. He listed the hallmarks of his suffering: five times he received 39 lashes, 195 total, three times he was beaten with rods, he received one stoning and endured three shipwrecks (2 Cor. 11:22-25). But he counts it all gain for Christ as he presses towards the high calling. There was something driving this man to push past pain, physical torture and endure self-denial. He was being transformed through the process and had the prize in sight.

Read Paul's instructions to the Romans:

> "So here's what I want you to do, God helping you: Take your everyday, ordinary life—your sleeping, eating, going-to-work, and walking-around life—and place it before God as an offering. Embracing what God does for you is the best thing you can do for him. Don't become so well-adjusted to your culture that you fit into it without even thinking. Instead, fix your attention on God. You'll be changed from the inside out. Readily recognize what he wants from you, and quickly respond to it. Unlike the culture around you, always dragging you down to its level of immaturity, God brings the best out of you, develops well-formed maturity in you."
>
> Romans 12:1-2 (MSG)

Once you have decided to be a disciple of Jesus, you now follow and devote yourself to your new training regimen. It is a life of discipline that earns you the title disciple. As a disciple you will be faced with many decisions, and exhibiting self-restraint and denial will become a significant part of your new identity.

Jesus calls us to live an overcoming life, and there is a special crown reserved for those who overcome. To be an overcomer means we have run our race, finished well and obtain our prize. Despite obstacles and opposition, we pressed through, running the race that is set before us.

COACHING

Anything we achieve in this life will require a price to be paid. Self-discipline is rooted in structure and repetition. Discipline encompasses adding new habits and deleting other useless, unproductive ones. The most accomplished athletes devote themselves to a training regimen requiring intense amounts of focus, discipline and self-denial. All top performers in their field, whether sports or business, have developed high-performance habits through consistent training and discipline.

It begins with mastering ourselves: acknowledge, break and remove old habits as we begin practicing restraint. Next, we'll install new actions and behaviors we've never taken before. Lastly, we'll add consistent repetition turning those actions into healthy habits that stick.

Jesus is a man of discipline. He decided to follow His Father's will, made a commitment and discipline fueled His purpose. What are you attempting to accomplish? What area do you need to be more disciplined in? Set your goal, decide what you want to achieve and use discipline as the vehicle to accomplish what you set out to do.

"I love those who love me, and those who seek me diligently will find me."

Proverbs 8:17 (NKJV)

JESUS IS DILIGENT

One of the hallmarks of anyone who has mastered their craft is diligence. To be diligent can be defined as: one who shows care in their work. It also carries the meaning of movement with decisive action and determination.

In the Bible the term 'diligence' is strongly correlated with work. It carries the picture of a sharp threshing instrument, which implies physical labor. There is a major theme of work woven throughout Scripture. Although He delivers us from many things, God does not deliver us from our work. He, Himself, modeled work starting in Genesis 1. God's plan for Jesus was for Him to work a blue-collar job for more than two thirds of His earthly life. It is here that Jesus had the opportunity to exhibit diligence. Operating in the daily grind, He kept His head down and focused on what God called Him to do with His assignment in that season.

> **Diligence is movement with decisive action and determination**

We all progress through seasons in our lives, and each season prepares us for the next. We learn and become something that will take us into the next season of life with more authority. Jesus was in His season of obscurity during the process of mastering His trade. His work as a builder prepared Him for His public ministry. I propose that Jesus carried out His day-to-day work as a tradesman with excellence. There is no doubt that He produced a superior product and offered great customer service.

> "Do you see a man who excels in his work? He will stand before kings; He will not stand before unknown men."
>
> Proverbs 22:29 (NKJV)

Another aspect of diligence is consistent movement towards your goal despite how you feel. Our emotions dictate how we feel, and they fluctuate daily. If we are operating based on our superficial desires and feelings, we will never attain our goals, master our craft or fulfill our assignment. Being diligent means taking action despite our present circumstances or feelings. If I only work when I feel like it, I will never pay the bills. If I only workout when I feel like it, I will never burn fat and build muscle. If I only write when I am inspired, this book would have never been finished. Jesus defends His yes to His father with no's to other things. He realizes by accepting His mission and embracing His purpose, it is mandatory that He denies the entry of nonessential things into His domain that could take Him away from His purpose. He had to say no in order to say yes. It is the same for us.

JESUS DEFENDS HIS YES TO HIS FATHER WITH NO'S TO DISTRACTIONS

Here are some things He says no to:

- He says no to hunger when He commits to fasting.
- He says no to laziness when He awakes early to pray.
- He says no to sleep when He stays up all night in prayer.
- He says no to the temptations that surround Him, so that He can say yes to God's plan.
- He says no to people who want to follow Him. Not everyone was allowed to travel with Him. He loves all, but instructed some to stay behind to influence their community.
- He says no to religious traditions, so He can say yes to His Father and heal on the Sabbath.
- He says no to Peter's request to avoid going to Jerusalem, so He can say yes to the cross.

JESUS PROTECTS HIS PURPOSE

Jesus used boundaries in His life to protect His purpose. He was loving, patient and endured the crowd's requests for teaching, preaching and healing all while guarding His purpose. He ministered to the crowds, but knew when to pull away. He healed the sick, but knew when His disciples needed deeper instruction. He was intentional in everything He did and still does.

He established daily habits, rituals and routines that nurtured and empowered His purpose. Jesus is our highest model for diligence. Jesus was diligent in all areas of life. For example, we read that early morning prayer was a daily habit. We see on multiple occasions that His day started and ended with a routine. It was common for Jesus to minister to the crowds, to seek solitude and to invest time in private coaching with His disciples. These are just some of the areas we will explore together as we uncover some of the powerful things Jesus models for us as men.

Morning rituals and routines are utilized by the most influential, successful and impactful people today. Jesus was no exception. He provides a template for us in His daily actions, habits and teachings. Success does not happen on accident, so to accomplish your mission and fulfill your calling, you will also need to be intentional in your daily actions. Consider a normal ritual in the life of Jesus:

> "And rising very early in the morning, while it was still dark, he departed and went out to a desolate place, and there he prayed."
>
> Mark 1:35

Jesus was diligent in His focus on His mission, which He defined as His 'work.' While mentoring His disciples in understanding their mission, He stated:

> "We must work the works of Him who sent Me as long as it is day; night is coming when no one can work."
>
> John 9:4

Another time after ministering to the crowds and observing the people overwhelmed by their troubles and wandering like sheep with no shepherd, He said to His disciples;

> "The harvest is plentiful, but the workers are few."
>
> Matthew 9:37

The theme of work in the life of Jesus did not stop when He entered public ministry. The ethic and excellence in His work remains the same while the day to day operations have changed in this season of ministry. King Solomon was the richest and wisest man in world history, and he writes this in the book of Proverbs on the subject of diligence in your work:

> "Poor is he who works with a negligent hand, but the hand of the diligent makes rich."
>
> Proverbs 10:4

> "The hand of the diligent will rule, but the slack hand will be put to forced labor."
>
> Proverbs 12:24

> "The soul of a lazy man desires, and has nothing; But the soul of the diligent shall be made rich."
>
> Proverbs 13:4 (NKJV)

> "The plans of the diligent lead surely to advantage, but everyone who is hasty comes surely to poverty."
>
> Proverbs 21:5

In Paul's letter to Timothy, we read the instruction of the Apostle to his mentee to:

> "...study to show yourself approved unto God, a workman that needs to not be ashamed."
>
> 2 Timothy 2:15

There is a correlation between diligence, work and faith that is inspired by the Lord and that He takes pleasure in.

> "But without faith it is impossible to please Him, for he who comes to God must believe that He is, and that He is a rewarder of those who diligently seek Him."
>
> Hebrews 11:6

COACHING

It is important to recognize the testing grounds God uses in our lives. All of the men that were used greatly of God went through periods of obscurity and ordinary circumstances, including Jesus. As men, we need to be diligent in our work. Throughout the Bible all men had a craft or trade they devoted themselves to. If their lineage did not include being part of the priesthood, they spent their lives honing a skill and mastering a trade that would contribute to the local economy and provide for their family. As an apprentice, they would learn diligence in their work and gain daily discipline learning from the master craftsman. There would no doubt be years of grunt work, ordinary and mundane activities.

Are you tired of daily grind? Maybe you're frustrated with your speed of growth and waiting for the next opportunity? Being diligent allows God to shape our character through the seemingly small and mundane work He has allowed us to do while we are in this season.

God is attracted to and blesses the work of the diligent and Jesus models diligence in all He does. The application for us as men is that we are to put all of our energy into the work that God has entrusted into our hands. This includes not only the passion projects when we are in our season of convergence, but also during the mundane, the ordinary and repetitive tasks while in our season of obscurity.

"But when you are invited, go and recline at the last place, so that when the one who has invited you comes, he may say to you, 'Friend, move up higher'; then you will have honor in the sight of all who are at the table with you."

Luke 14:10

JESUS DEMONSTRATES RESTRAINT

Jesus lived a life of self-control and was never moved from His center to react emotionally, or lose control of his mental and emotional state as a man. There are numerous times He would be tested and tried by His natural surroundings and situations. The Pharisees were a continuous thorn in His side. Do you think you have haters in your life? They stalked Him, scheming and seeking to capture Him in a moment of weakness. Despite their traps and taunts Jesus never responded by exhibiting pride or ego. At any moment during His mission on earth He could have abandoned His call. Instead He chose the path of humility because of His consuming love for us – this is the driving force fueling all of His decisions. He never moved in His flesh to 'one up' an accuser or prove who He is. He is firm in His identity and uses discretion when choosing His responses to life's circumstances.

Jesus modeled humility and restraint. He also imparts this value to His followers. Jesus instructed them (and us) by stating, "Don't cast your pearls before swine." There is no need to show or prove who you are all the time. Only the insecure and ego-driven feel the need to seek the recognition of men. Many times, after healing someone, He instructed them not to openly tell who healed them (Mark 1:44). He was not seeking fame or recognition for the miracles He performed.

My point here is one of restraint: don't be presumptuous in the positioning of yourself. It is far better to remain humble and allow the king to invite you at your appointed time than to pre-maturely seek the validation and recognition of others.

The Lord's instruction and model for us is to have discretion. Just because you can, does not mean you should. Just because you have the gift, office or title, does not require you to use it, demonstrate it or put it on full display at all times. It is the immature and insecure who boast about what they have accomplished and are capable of. The mature man's confidence comes from identity, not gifting, possessions or status.

Our identity in Christ is rooted in our sonship, not our gifts, skills or titles. When you are secure in your identity as a son of God, you will start to act differently. When the revelation of who you are in Christ is embraced, your internal security will shift from spiritual giftings, natural abilities and status, to resting in knowing who you are as a son. Sometimes this security and understanding of your identity in Christ causes insecurities to be exposed in those around you. Jesus causes a reaction from the religiously insecure. This happened whenever He crossed paths with the religious order. He was not threatened or pulled into petty arguments over someone else's insecurity. He very clearly knows who He is, and His restraint testifies of His identity.

Your confidence in your God-given identity will cause the insecurities of those around you to be exposed.

In Matthew 13:52, Jesus shares a parable of the wealthy home owner; someone who has new and old treasures. The wealthy man uses discretion on when to present the old or the new treasures. Just because you can bring out your treasure, does not mean you always should. A true disciple demonstrates self-mastery, which encompasses the ability to show restraint and self-regulate.

Jesus was born a human, He shared the same flesh and blood we do. We have little record of the first early years of Jesus life but we are very clear on what his mission was. His primary purpose was to seek and save the lost. We know exactly when He stepped onto the scene in the fulfillment of His ministry calling. When He steps into the Jordan River, wading out in the water towards John the Baptist, He is fulfilling righteousness,

Old Testament prophecy and stepping into His destiny. It was 30 years of restraint for three years of public ministry; 30 years of knowing who He is with His purpose submitted to the perfect will and timing of His Father. Jesus is our model for self-mastery. Jesus plays His position perfectly and executes flawlessly, never jumping the gun, exhibiting a false start or stepping out of alignment with His calling.

King Solomon recorded these wise words in Proverbs:

> "Do not claim honor in the presence of the king, and do not stand in the place of great men; For it is better that it be said to you, 'Come up here,' than for you to be placed lower in the presence of the prince, whom your eyes have seen."
>
> Proverbs 25:6-7

Similarly, Jesus said:

> "But when you are invited, go and sit in the lowest place, so that when your host comes he may say to you, 'Friend, move up higher.' Then you will be honored in the presence of all who sit at the table with you."
>
> Luke 14:10

COACHING

Men are designed with purpose. Our inner drive is hard wired to pursue greatness and achievement. Seeking God's wisdom fuels our ability to fulfill our calling. When we are unsure or confused, we'll seek to run after what we feel we are supposed to pursue, often not fully knowing what we are trying to accomplish. Running with no clearly-defined destination or map of how to get there requires massive amounts of energy and usually ends up in burn out. It is us trying to apprehend something we desire out of season. I love the story of when Jesus sent two of His disciples to the town ahead, providing them instructions on how to secure His source of transport for His triumphant entry into Jerusalem.

> "Go into the village ahead of you; there, as you enter, you will find a colt tied on which no one yet has ever sat; untie it and bring it here. If anyone asks you, 'Why are you untying it?' you shall say, 'The Lord has need of it.'"
>
> Luke 19:30

This is a perfect picture of how exhibiting restraint in your life can interplay with God's call, assignment and destiny for you. At times we all feel like that donkey, tied to a post watching everyone pass us by, never thinking our day will come. The beauty in this scene is that Jesus, sovereignly in His perfect time and your assigned season, sends for you. He arranges the circumstances to align perfectly and it is impossible to miss His opportunity for your life.

"Immediately the Spirit impelled Him to go out into the wilderness."

Mark 1:12

JESUS HAS A PLAN

After entering public ministry signified by His baptism in the Jordan, Jesus immediately departs for the wilderness where He fasts for 40 days. Fasting for this amount of time requires an incredible amount of discipline, self-control and commitment. A key that we can receive from Jesus is that He is not acting spontaneously. Some planning went into where He would go following His entrance into public ministry. I propose that He had already determined He would be fasting for the next 40 days. He had prepared Himself spiritually, mentally, emotionally and physically for what would occur for over the next month (Mark 1:12,13). Jesus is a planner.

He removes Himself from temptation. He does not enter a fast of this length in the marketplace surrounded by distractions and temptations. He separates Himself from the view of things that could compromise His plan. Jesus departs for the wilderness. Separation is a key to preparation.

The gospel of Luke captures the account of the temptation of Jesus. In Luke 4:1-4 we read;

> "Jesus, full of the Holy Spirit, returned from the Jordan and was led around by the Spirit in the wilderness for forty days, being tempted by the devil. And He ate nothing during those days, and when they had ended, He became hungry. And the devil said to Him, "If You are the Son of God, tell this stone to become bread." And Jesus answered him, "It is written, 'Man shall not live on bread alone.'"
>
> Luke 4:1-4

After His 40-day fast, Jesus is in a physically-vulnerable state when Satan the tempter arrives. Jesus employs discipline and devotion to His Father and their mission together by utterly rejecting the offer of food, power and praise.

Satan will tempt Jesus, appealing to three appetites that all men crave. First, he will appeal to the physical, in this case man's basic need for food. Despite being in a nutritionally-depleted state, Jesus does not compromise and defeats Satan with the Word of God. Jesus declares, "Man will not live by bread alone…" and this statement pierces Satan in a failed attempt to compromise His mission.

Next, Satan appeals to the soul realm of man and tempts Jesus with an appeal for influence, ambition and worldly success on earth.

> "And he led Him up and showed Him all the kingdoms of the world in a moment of time. And the devil said to Him, "I will give You all this domain and its glory; for it has been handed over to me, and I give it to whomever I wish. Therefore if You worship before me, it shall all be Yours." Jesus answered him, "It is written, 'You shall worship the Lord your God and serve Him only.'"
>
> Luke 4:5-8

Jesus overcomes the enemy and with authority states, *"It is written…"* His words once again leave Satan reaching for another angle.

Lastly, Satan appeals to the spirit realm of man and tempts Jesus to step out of His calling and identity as the Messiah, by exercising His power to prove who He is.

> "And he led Him to Jerusalem and had Him stand on the pinnacle of the temple, and said to Him, "If You are the Son of God, throw Yourself down from here; for it is written,
> 'HE will command His angels concerning You to guard You,' and,
> 'ON their hands they will bear You up,
> SO that You will not strike Your foot against A stone.'"
> And Jesus answered and said to him, "It is said, 'You shall not put the Lord your God to the test.'"
> When the devil had finished every temptation, he left Him until an opportune time."
>
> Luke 4:9-13

"It is written…" is proclaimed from the mouth of a physically-exhausted,

yet spiritually-strong Jesus. His rebuke leaves Satan defeated, but Satan is determined to return again at a more opportune time.

Separation is a key to preparation

We can learn about our enemy's strategy by how he launched this attack on Jesus. Let's take a closer look at the three domains Satan focuses his energy on in this assault. It is important to understand the strategy behind this attack, because we will also be tempted in all of these areas. To live a life that overcomes we must be aware of our enemy.

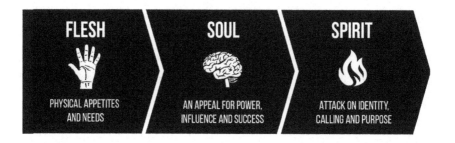

FLESH

This is the pattern of attack, and flesh is first. Most men will fail at the first level of attack where our enemy appeals to our basic physical appetites, and five senses – what the Bible refers to as the lust of the flesh or lust of the eyes. This can encompass lust for women, the temptation to engage in sexual activity that crosses the boundary of what God has set for us outside of a healthy marriage. It also applies to our physical appetites and addictions with food and alcohol, as well as the lust for material possessions.

SOUL

Next, we see the attack on the soul realm. This is the realm that comprises our consciousness: our mind, will and emotions. Here is where an appeal to our status, pride and ego happens. These are the things of the world which the Bible describes as the pride of life. In this case, the attack has to do with an internal battle, and the appeal of worldly status is an external force that can compromise us internally. This attack appeals to our human ambition to accomplish more, receive more and be more.

SPIRIT

The realm of our spirit is the part of us that is eternal. The spirit of a man (for a born-again believer) is regenerated, made alive and seated in heavenly places in Christ. The third tactic was where the enemy made an appeal for worship, attacking our identity, calling and purpose.

Jesus cannot be moved off of His mark; He does not waver and will not compromise. As men, we are faced with temptations every day on every front. John gives us this warning:

> "Don't set the affections of your heart on this world or in loving the things of the world. The love of the Father and the love of the world are incompatible. For all that the world can offer us—the gratification of our flesh, the allurement of the things of the world, and the obsession with status and importance —none of these things come from the Father but from the world. This world and its desires are in the process of passing away, but those who love to do the will of God live forever."
>
> 1 John 2-15-17 (TPT)

Jesus' strength came from His devotion and intimacy with the Father. Discipline flows from devotion.

We are born into a battle. Our spiritual enemy roams like a roaring lion seeking who he can devour. He is patient and often attacks when we are at our weakest, and even when we overcome, he departs for a season, determined to return when we are at a low point in life. We know the enemy re-visited Jesus later in His ministry prior to the cross. The devil launched an attack strategically at the lowest times in Jesus' life: when He was alone, hungry and abandoned by His friends.

Discipline flows from devotion

Jesus was tempted by the devil and we read that the devil left him…for a season. This implies we, too, will be tempted in an on-going fashion. We must be filled with the Spirit to resist and overcome the enemy and be empowered for our assignment. The devil manifested to Jesus right before Jesus launched His ministry of miracles and mighty works. Temptations are strategically tied to ministry, mission and power.

Living a life with clarity of purpose is rooted in knowing our identity and calling. Waking up day after day and 'going with the flow' will never lead to a life that overcomes. If we are to reach and fulfill our destiny, purpose and calling, being firmly rooted in our identity is critical. How did Jesus overcome the devil? He does not waver in who He is or what He came to do. He knows His ultimate purpose.

We overcome in the same manner. We must know our true identity – the one we are called to be. We must be rooted in our purpose, unshakeable in who Jesus says we are. If there is one thing I know for sure, you are called to be an overcomer. Jesus overcame with the Word of God. Jesus is the Word made flesh. Each time He was confronted, He prefaced His response with, "It is written…" Jesus lets the Word answer the attack of the enemy. When we know the Word, we can use the Word against the enemy when we are tempted. The Word is our spiritual sword to go on the offensive with.

Temptations are strategically tied to ministry, mission and power

COACHING

We are called to be in the world and not of it. Part of that call means we are to carry light everywhere we go. But, it does not mean that we have to completely separate ourselves, not engaging with culture and retreating into our private community for fear of being tempted. Temptations will always be present. There is wisdom in being self-aware of those things that easily beset us. My battle with sin and temptation may differ from your battle. When we are aware of unhealthy desires on a physical, soulish and spiritual level, we can be proactive to address those.

This can look like avoiding a location, people or things that make us prone to temptation or position us for a fall. We must always be looking forward, ready to conquer our day. As Jesus models for us, this will require a plan. Be intentional about how you set your course. As kings and priests, we make moves purposefully; moves that flow out of devotion to our Father.

"I must preach the kingdom of God to the other cities also, for I was sent for this purpose."

Luke 4:43

JESUS IS CONFIDENT IN HIS IDENTITY

Jesus knows who He is and what He is called to do. When He entered into His public ministry and made the transition from obscurity to being embraced as a celebrity, He chose to read Isaiah's prophecy, which details the character, mission and attributes of the Messiah. He fully identifies and embraces this word by publicly declaring it and announcing its fulfillment – a dangerous proposition in His hometown of Nazareth. Below is a portion of the scroll that Jesus would have read from.

> Isaiah 61
> The Spirit of the Lord God is upon me,
> Because the Lord has anointed me
> To bring good news to the afflicted;
> He has sent me to bind up the brokenhearted,
> To proclaim liberty to captives
> And freedom to prisoners;
> To proclaim the favorable year of the Lord
> And the day of vengeance of our God;
> To comfort all who mourn,
> To grant those who mourn in Zion,
> Giving them a garland instead of ashes,
> The oil of gladness instead of mourning,
> The mantle of praise instead of a spirit of fainting.
> So they will be called oaks of righteousness,
> The planting of the Lord, that He may be glorified.

Jesus was not driven by ego and opposes the proud. He exercises meekness and values humility. He does not suffer from false humility, an identity crisis or sheepishly accepting who He is. He is strong, He is clear and He is confident about His identity.

The backdrop of this account is that Jesus was teaching at the synagogue in His hometown of Nazareth. Those in the crowd would have consisted of His relatives, neighbors, friends of His family and those who would have known Him growing up as a boy who shadowed Joseph as an apprentice in the family business. The bible records that the listeners were astonished by His wisdom and the miracles He performed. The crowd's admiration quickly turned into shock and anger with a tone of "Who does He think He is?" Jesus' discernment and emotional intelligence prompts the following statement, "A prophet is not without honor except in his hometown and among his own relatives and in his own household" (Mark 6:4). Luke's account tells us that offense quickly turned to rage, and the crowd actually drove Him out to a hill where their intention was to throw Him off a cliff, but Jesus passed through them and went on His way.

In this story, Jesus teaches us that it is those who are most familiar with you who may not understand your calling, mission and assignment. It was necessary for Jesus to immediately depart His hometown to launch His ministry away from those who could only relate to Him in one, old way. The other lesson we see is that even when He is fulfilling His ministry mandate, He cannot stay where He is not honored. He will later teach this principle to His followers as He sends them out into the world with the instruction to shake the dust from their feet if a town rejects them.

The core principle He shares here is that to thrive in your mission and assignment, you may have to leave behind familiar places and relationships with people who choose to be offended with what you are pursuing. Jesus does not tolerate those who want to kill His mission. Jesus does not feel the need to defend, engage in intellectual debates or argue over His identity. He speaks the truth with love and moves on. Throughout His ministry He would be tested in many ways, yet He never backed down, was not deterred from His mission and did not succumb to sin.

JESUS GOES WHERE HE IS CELEBRATED, NOT WHERE HE IS TOLERATED

In an exchange with the religious leaders on one occasion, He stated plainly:

> "I have no need to be validated by men, but I'm saying these things so that you will believe and be rescued."
> John 5:34 (TPT)

Jesus did not suffer from an identity crisis. He was absolutely clear on His purpose and mandate. He did not need the validation of man or the respect of others. They could not appeal to His flesh to pull Him into an argument for the sake of defending His identity out of pride, He remains humble and He always speaks the truth and never apologizes for who He is.

On another occasion Jesus said:

> "I am light to the world and those who embrace me will experience life-giving light, and they will never walk in darkness."
> John 8:12 (TPT)

Look at what unfolds following this revelation from the mouth of Jesus:

> "The Pharisees were immediately offended and said, 'You're just boasting about yourself! Since we only have your word on this, it makes your testimony invalid!' Jesus responded, 'Just because I am the one making these claims doesn't mean they're invalid. For I absolutely know who I am, where I've come from, and where I'm going.'"
> John 8:13-14 (TPT)

CLARITY AND INTENTIONALITY

Later in His ministry, Jesus reveals to His disciples that He must be put to death. One of his best friends, Peter, tries to dissuade him. With strong words rooted in firm conviction, Peter's visceral response to this revelation is, *"Jesus, this will not be so!"* Peter is speaking out of his natural mind with no spiritual awareness of what must happen for Jesus to fulfill His assignment. He does not realize his words are an attempt to extinguish the very purposes of God.

Jesus rebukes Satan who is using Peter at this moment in an attempt to cancel the calling and fulfillment of Jesus' mission (Matt. 4:10). Jesus has no need to smooth over others' comments. He does not ignore them, play nice or avoid awkward and uncomfortable situations. He confronts and corrects, bringing light where there is no understanding and alignment to thinking that is out of order.

In the final days of his earthly life, the Roman guards, heavily outfitted in their battle dress, armed with swords, are led to the garden of Gethsemane by Judas the betrayer. Jesus confronts the Roman soldiers by asking who they are looking for. When they state His name, He confidently steps forward and declares so all can hear:

"I AM HE"

This ownership of who He is leaves the Romans so stunned that they back pedal, tripping on each other and fall down in the presence of an unarmed Jesus (John 18:1-9).

HE KNOWS WHO HE IS

COACHING

THE PRESENT-DAY IDENTITY CRISIS

For many men an internal identity crisis and battle is fought daily. Insecurity, false humility or being ashamed to embrace your identity due to a fear of pride will never allow you to function in your calling and assignment. If Jesus acted this way, He would be incapable of His mission. There are three common major lies that attack us on the way to our destiny. It is important to recognize if you are exhibiting these conditions and deal with them immediately. Our enemy wants to see us vacate our assignment and abandon our calling. Below are three limitations that seek to stop you from functioning in your identity.

INSECURITY

Peter, after His public denial of Jesus, was unsure of who he was, was unsure of his calling and questioned his capacity to serve in it. He was a strong-willed, stubborn man who forged his own way in life by will power, grit and grind. We cannot function in our true calling by sheer force or hustle. No matter how hard Peter works in his own strength, he cannot find his identity apart from Jesus. When he fails publicly by denying his Lord, he is lost, broken and insecure. It is at this point when he fell into despair, feeling like a failure. It wasn't until after his restoration through an encounter with Jesus that he could boldly proclaim Christ, and then emerged in leadership among the newly-formed church.

Jesus defines who Peter is; Jesus calls Peter and gives him mission, mandate and power to accomplish his call. Like Peter, if you are unsure of what you are called to do in the Kingdom, you will wrestle with dissatisfaction and lack of identity. It will feel like an internal tug of war where you want to go, but do not feel ready, able or confident. The enemy seeks to make us insecure, because insecurity is the place where we are paralyzed. The answer for Peter was an encounter with Jesus. The answer is the same for us.

PRIDE AND EGO

Saul of Tarsus was one of the most well-studied and accomplished Pharisees of his day. He could not come to Jesus or be used by Him because he was driven by his ego and held back by his pride. Saul's confidence came from his intellect and the honor and respect he received from man. Lack of humility kept Saul from seeking the truth about Jesus. One day, on his way to persecute the early church, Saul had an encounter with Jesus on the road to Damascus and emerges as Paul. Jesus gives him a new identity with a new name. As a result of this experience, Paul loses his physical sight for a time and travels to the wilderness where his pride is stripped away before being mightily used in ministry and fulfilling his calling.

The methods God uses when He calls a man have not changed. We see a clear pattern throughout the Bible of how God deals with a man before He uses him. Pride in our natural abilities and our status must be broken off on the road to our new identity in Christ. Before God uses anything or anyone, He breaks it first. Maintaining purity empowers you to unlock your calling and be entrusted with the power to fulfill your assignment, God will break you of your trust in yourself, the seeking of praise from others and desire to be esteemed by men. Pride, whether spiritual or natural, will hold you back from walking into the fullness of your assignment. It was necessary for Paul to have an encounter with

Jesus prior to public ministry, and it is necessary for us as well.

FALSE HUMILITY

False humility manifests in a number of ways, including making internal comparisons to those around you. As men we love to size each other up when meeting someone for the first time. The normal starting question is, "What do you do for a living?" By assessing this information, a measuring system emerges based on the worldview and values you live by. If money is your number one determinant of success, then you may assert status over another because you have more. If you measure your own success by how much is in your bank account, then you will immediately feel weakened when meeting a higher net-worth individual.

Christian men are not immune from this behavior. We often fall into the comparison trap as well. This can include being intimidated by those who you deem as having superior gifting, a higher calling or more developed skill sets. False humility could have us use self-deprecation to receive compliments. But, genuine humility seeks to honor and esteem others first, lift up those around us and look to support our brothers who are running in the same direction.

Another manifestation of false humility can be altering who you are to mute your gifts and talents to those around you. This is also based in comparison or not wanting to make others around us feel less than us, so we change how we show up and play at a lower level. This can look like tamping down our gift or holding back on our true identity and call because of the fear of man or fear of making those around you feel inferior or less secure. The truth is, changing who you are to cater to a perceived insecurity in another never

COACHING

brings freedom to you or those around you.

Jesus was secure in His identity, clear in His purpose and confident in His mission. He had compassion for those who He crossed paths with – even those who had the pride of life, whether overtly paraded in public or covertly masquerading as false humility. Jesus also led his team in a way where they all esteemed and honored each other. From my personal experience, men often struggle with comparison within their peer group.

"Therefore Pilate said to Him, 'So You are a king?' Jesus answered, 'You say correctly that I am a king. For this I have been born, and for this I have come into the world, to testify to the truth. Everyone who is of the truth hears My voice.'"

John 18:37-38

JESUS WON'T BE CONFINED TO MAN'S DEFINITION

The nation of Israel had a promise, image and expectation of the Messiah. They have a long history of being controlled by other nations, starting with Egypt found in the Exodus account. They gain their freedom from the physical slavery of Pharaoh and are shown a promised land that the Lord has reserved as an inheritance for them. Despite the promise, they will have to fight for every parcel of land. Throughout the record of the Old Testament, we observe a constant struggle with enemy nations as well as God's discipline that is used to bring them back to Himself. Fast forward to the times of Jesus, and Israel is expecting a Messiah who would deliver them from the oppressive rule of Rome.

Their interpretation of the scriptures pointed to a deliverer, a Messiah who would rescue Israel and usher in a new era for their nation. The Jewish people were on the lookout for an overcomer. Every Jewish family would have told stories of this coming deliverer as they gathered around the dinner table. The religious institution had high expectations of a conquering Messiah who would become their king on the earth. There was also a politically-motivated sect known as the Zealots, who were revolutionary nationalists in their attitude and violent in their behavior towards the Roman occupation of their land. These Zealots expected a Messiah who would cause a political uprising and overthrow their oppressive Roman occupiers. The two driving forces in Israel during this time period were the religious order and the political class. The religious order didn't understand Jesus and were threatened by Him and His message, while the politically-motivated Zealots sought a way to control Jesus and use Him to fit their agenda.

Today we have a similar wrestling match over Jesus and His message. The setting and time period have changed, but the driving forces behind the religious and political mindsets have not. Many groups attempted to use Jesus to position and strengthen their message...enter the social justice warriors, the extreme left as well as the extreme right, all fighting to lay claim to Jesus as the banner for their beliefs. Jesus cannot be manipulated to fit into others agendas. He will not be used by man and refuses to be confined to anyone's definition.

One night when the disciples were gathered around Jesus, they started sharing stories of how the crowds are referring to Him. As they recount the list of the names, titles and people that Jesus is being compared to, Jesus calls upon Peter with a question that echoes through the pages of the Bible.

"WHO DO YOU SAY THAT I AM?"

Jesus cuts through the noise, empty banter and having to fulfill any expectation that man places upon Him with this challenging question that not only Peter will be faced with, but we as well. This question is not rhetorical. It is not mere words occupying empty space in a conversation. This question demands a response from us all.

In this exchange, Jesus shares His plans to enter Jerusalem and prophecies of what He must do. His plan includes betrayal, being placed into the hands of Rome and ultimately death. Jesus disrupts all of the pre-conceived ideas and does not fit into any of the boxes or definitions that men tried to label Him with. According to Isaiah's prophecies, Jesus was to be the suffering servant, born into the lowliest of conditions, raised in a working-class family and from an obscure town. Jesus models unprecedented servant leadership, a King who acts like a servant. This was very different than the warring conqueror that Israel was hoping for and they rejected Jesus and his message because of it.

> "He came to His own, and those who were His own did not receive Him."
>
> John 1:11

He does speak of establishing His Kingdom and uses radical language and preaches an uncompromising message that most are uncomfortable with. It still does not fit the people's expectations of the Messiah. He talks in a way that is in direct opposition with all of their hopes and dreams of a physical deliverance. "Turn the other cheek," and "If your neighbor asks for your shirt give him your coat also," (Matt 5:40) and "Love your neighbor as yourself" (Mark 12:31). This is not the rhetoric of a political revolutionary or that of a religious king.

Jesus did, in fact, come to end oppression, to offer deliverance, to overcome and establish a new Kingdom rule. Israel missed the time of their deliverance. Why? Because they had hopes of a natural deliverance from their present-day circumstances. Jesus offers deliverance from sin and spiritual freedom. When Pilate asked Him if He was King of the Jews, Jesus responds:

> "…My kingdom is not of this world. If My kingdom were of this world, then My servants would be fighting so that I would not be handed over to the Jews; but as it is, My kingdom is not of this realm."
>
> John 18:36

Everywhere Jesus went He spread the message of the Kingdom.

COACHING

How have people labeled you throughout your life? From the time we are boys we receive labels. I remember my first-grade teacher told my mother at the parent teacher conference that I was a "chatterbox." It's interesting how I can still recall the exact 'label' the teacher assigned me.

Throughout our lives our parents, teachers and managers label us by identifying us with the traits they see in us. These spoken words can be incredibly powerful in forming our identity and the view we have of ourselves. As we learned from the life of Jesus, He did not allow others to negatively define Him or impact His mission.

It is important for us to be open to receiving feedback. We should be available to listen, accept and make course corrections based on the wisdom of others. However, we need to be able to discern the motives and intentions of those who would attempt to minimize us, our mission and our dreams with an incorrect label. When Peter defined and declared who Jesus was to Him, he stepped into his destiny. When you define and declare who Jesus is to you, you will align with your assignment with more clarity and power. Our identity is directly shaped by the way we view God in our life. The first step to becoming clear about your identity is to clearly define who Jesus is in your life.

"Jesus left the upper room with his disciples and, as was his habit, went to the Mount of Olives, his place of secret prayer."

Luke 22:39 (TPT)

JESUS IS A MAN OF PRAYER

Scripture records that Jesus prayed often. Have you ever wondered why Jesus, the Son of God, fully equal with God the Father, prays to His Father? Jesus came to earth as man and although fully God, He was also fully man. Because of this, He can relate to the human condition on every level, other than the exception that He never missed the mark by giving in to sin. As the Son of Man, He was accessing God through His humanity. Prayer is a spiritual experience that we as humans can enter into, and it is the act of exercising His spiritual connection through His human flesh that Jesus models for us.

Jesus prays before every major event and decision in His life, and here are just a few examples:

- Before He raised Lazarus from the dead (John 11:41-42)
- When He entered Jerusalem (John 12:27-28)
- In the garden of Gethsemane (Matt 26:36, John 17)
- Jesus prays while He is on the cross (Luke 23:34, 46, Matt 27:46, Mark 15:34)

He also prays as part of His daily practice when there are no major events mentioned.

> "But Jesus Himself would often slip away to the wilderness and pray."
> Luke 5:16

He prayed prayers that covered many areas of life. A few examples are:

- Prayers of thanksgiving
- Prayers for His disciples
- Prayers for all believers
- Prayers when His soul is troubled

Even more than these, prayer was His way of life. It was common practice for Jesus to seclude Himself in early morning prayer. As He traveled the Middle East as an itinerant minister, the location would change, but His morning routine would remain consistent. Early morning prayer appears to be routine in the life of Jesus. Luke records the following:

> "At daybreak the next morning, the crowds came and searched everywhere for him, but Jesus had already left to go to a secluded place."
> Luke 4:42a

The pattern of prayer in the life of Jesus is a consistent theme, and His prayer time was not limited to mornings only. Another common practice of Jesus was to spend the evening in prayer.

> "After this, Jesus went up into the high hills to spend the whole night in prayer to God."
> Luke 6:12 (TPT)

Brian Simmons notes in The Passion Translation that; "This was the pattern of Jesus in the Gospel accounts. Before he made important decisions and before great events in his life, he sought the Father. Once he saw what the Father wanted, Jesus obeyed as the perfect Son." (TPT note C, Luke 6:12)

Jesus models intimacy with His Father. Jesus stated that He only does what He sees His Father doing. As He emerges from His place of prayer in the morning and sets out for a day of teaching and ministry, Jesus already knew what the day would bring, who He would be speaking to and what they needed. This knowledge flowed through the Holy Spirit from His constant communion with His Father (John 5:19).

Jesus understands the role of habits to master Himself

YOUR MORNING ROUTINE

Although we have records of Jesus praying at all times of the day, we clearly observe that He had a morning routine. He developed daily disciplines and built habits that shaped His character and aligned Him to His mission.

In John 15:14, Jesus states to His disciples: "You are My friends if you do what I command you." "The Greek verb here indicates if you keep on obeying as a habit" (TPT note J, John 15:14). Bible scholar Kenneth Wuest translates it this way in the Wuest translation:

> "As for you, friends of mine you are, if you habitually do that which I am enjoining upon you."

Rituals and routine play an important role in the lives of all high performers regardless of the sport, industry or mission.

In 'Jesus is Diligent', we briefly discussed what Jesus' life looked like as He demonstrated diligence through his work. His day-to-day activities would have consisted of projects He looked forward to, as well as tasks that had become mundane during years of repetition. His attitude, thoughts and emotions may have run the spectrum of the emotions we all experience towards work. There are times when you feel like working and there are days you don't. Discipline is developed through showing up on the days when you don't feel like it. Success is found in the diligence to do what is required regardless of the cost. Jesus understands the role of habits to master Himself. He developed these disciplines and high-performance habits over the course of His entire life. He employed the power accumulated through these daily disciplines to fulfill His mission.

Like a well-trained athlete, Jesus had trained before official game time. He put in the practice to develop strength, power, endurance and capacity.

COACHING

Most men struggle with quiet time because we don't know the best way to approach God in prayer. There are approaches and templates we can use in our daily application of this discipline. Here a few ways to get started developing an effective prayer habit.

There is something about giving God the best part of your day and initiating the day with time spent in the Lord's presence. David said,

> "Early in the morning will I seek you"
> Psalm 63:1 (NKJV)

The goal of prayer is not just to speak, but also to listen. Developing spiritual listening skills through biblical meditation and contemplation on the scriptures is valuable. Many people have a difficult time learning to quiet their mind, being silent and waiting upon the Lord. Start with reading a Christ-centered scripture or portion of a chapter and allow each word to settle deep into your spirit as you focus your attention on Jesus.

If you want to get a framework to build a daily discipline of prayer in your life visit kingdomdrivenman.com

"Come to Me, all who are weary and heavy-laden, and I will give you rest. Take My yoke upon you and learn from Me, for I am gentle and humble in heart, and you will find rest for your souls. For My yoke is easy and My burden is light."

Matthew 11:28

JESUS VALUES BEING ALONE

A model Jesus provides us with is the value of solitude. Jesus loves people. The majority of His ministry was spent laboring among the crowds. Scripture records that He healed all who were oppressed. He stayed, taught and talked with the ordinary, the rejected and downtrodden. A pattern we see in the life of Jesus is Him giving out sacrificially during times of ministry, not holding back. He stays and labors fulfilling His Isaiah 61 mission:

- Proclaim good tidings to the poor
- Heal the sick
- Unlock prison doors
- Declare freedom to the oppressed

He carries, releases and demonstrates the Kingdom of God everywhere He goes.

THERE ARE TIMES WHERE HE PULLS AWAY TO BE ALONE

Though He loved the people, He also placed a priority on isolation from the demanding crowds. After these times of public ministry, we can find Jesus escaping the crowds to rest and spend time alone. He often taught His disciples after public ministry, answering their questions or explaining the hidden meanings of the things He shared with the crowds. After these busy times, it was not uncommon for Jesus to depart and find time to be alone.

> "After He had sent the crowds away, He went up on the mountain by Himself to pray; and when it was evening, He was there alone."
> Matt 14:23

> "In the early morning, while it was still dark, Jesus got up, left the house, and went away to a secluded place, and was praying there. Simon and his companions searched for Him; they found Him, and said to Him, 'Everyone is looking for You.'"
>
> Mark 1:35

In the above passage, the fact that the disciples and crowds were searching for Him implies He must have been gone for a while, spending a considerable amount of time alone in prayer.

After the death of John the Baptist, Jesus went to be alone.

> "Now when Jesus heard about John, He withdrew from there in a boat to a secluded place by Himself…"
>
> Matt 14:13

It was common for Jesus to climb a mountain or go to a high place to find seclusion and pray.

> "Departing from there, Jesus went along by the Sea of Galilee, and having gone up on the mountain, He was sitting there."
>
> Matthew 15:29

> "…while He Himself was sending the crowd away. After bidding them farewell, He left for the mountain to pray."
>
> Mark 6:45-46

Jesus taught the crowds about prayer. He describes prayer in an intimate manner, a private time in the secret place, out of sight, away from the crowds, where you can enter into 1:1 communion.

> "But you, when you pray, go into your inner room, close your door and pray to your Father who is in secret, and your Father who sees what is done in secret will reward you."
>
> Matthew 6:6

Although being alone and finding solitude is a practice Jesus gave priority to, we observe Jesus act with tremendous grace when interrupted or pressed with the need of man around Him. He was often interrupted in His private time with His disciples, while He is alone and often while He was eating (Mark 6:31), yet He always acted with patience and grace.

> "Months later, the apostles returned from their ministry tour and told Jesus all the wonders and miracles they had witnessed. Jesus, wanting to be alone with the Twelve, quietly slipped away with them toward Bethsaida. But the crowds soon found out about it and took off after him. When they caught up with Jesus, he graciously welcomed them all, taught them more about God's kingdom realm, and healed all who were sick."
>
> Luke 9:10-11 (TPT)

COACHING

Intentionality and purpose are always present with Jesus. As our leader He models the way for us. His actions show us that if you value something, you make time for it. Prioritizing time to seek solitude was a non-negotiable in the life of Jesus. As men we are constantly challenged with time constraints and demands on our productivity. Between balancing our family and work, there never seem to be enough hours in the day. It will never be easy to 'find' the time to pray, study and meditate in the Word. Jesus shows us you don't find time, you create it. He would arise and depart the village in the early hours; so early the crowds would not have noticed He was missing. He didn't advertise His time alone, as it was sacred and necessary in His life. When discovered, He displayed patience and grace, quickly transitioning to meet the needs of those around Him.

As a father of three children, I have found that the only time when I can truly be alone is in the early morning hours before everyone awakes. In the previous chapter we discussed more about the necessity of an early-morning routine. Regardless of the actual time of day, we can view the value Jesus places on solitude and time spent alone with the Father.

"Again, the devil took Him to a very high mountain and showed Him all the kingdoms of the world and their glory; and he said to Him, 'All these things I will give You, if You fall down and worship me.' Then Jesus said to him, 'Go, Satan! For it is written, 'You shall worship the Lord your God, and serve Him only.'"

Matthew 4:8-10

JESUS DOES NOT COMPROMISE

Jesus faced many pressures throughout His earthly life and was tempted in every way just as we are as men. He faced the temptations of His youth, the peer pressure of His day and experienced the same emotions common to all men living out their human existence.

Throughout this time, He never missed the mark. He stayed true to His calling and maintained focus with single-eye vision, overcoming temptations and living in obedience to the will of His Father. Jesus entered experientially into the feelings of our human condition, and Jesus understands our humanity. The writer of Hebrews states it this way:

> "For we do not have a high priest who cannot sympathize with our weaknesses, but One who has been tempted in all things as we are, yet without sin."
>
> Hebrews 4:15

Before Jesus launched His public ministry, John the Baptist was paving the way and gathering attention with an uncompromising message of repentance announcing the coming of the Messiah. The standard that John pronounced was one of uncompromising holiness.

> "…He will submerge you into union with the Spirit of Holiness and with a raging fire! He comes with a winnowing fork in his hands and comes to his threshing floor to sift what is worthless from what is pure. And he is ready to sweep out his threshing floor and gather his wheat into his granary, but the straw he will burn up with a fire that can't be extinguished!"
>
> Matthew 3:11-12 (TPT)

There was no wavering with John's definition of what living holy means. He paints the picture of an all-consuming fire that burns within our hearts for the Lord. John the Baptist was an Essene, part of a sect that separated themselves from society. John himself lived an uncompromising life that did not conform to the mainstream of his day. John would have been considered strange, as a man who lived in caves in the wilderness, wore a camel hair garment and lived on a diet consisting of locusts and wild honey.

Shortly after John makes his prophetic pronouncement of the One who is to come after him, Jesus is baptized by John and immediately departs for the wilderness. We have already observed Jesus as a man who moves with strong intention and executes His plan by preparation. He was prepared for separation, prepared for His 40-day fast and even for temptation. The standard Jesus sets is one of no compromise, which He expects from all those who follow Him. In the book of Revelation, Jesus communicates a message to the church of Laodicea. Jesus uses strong language to rebuke this church because they have allowed the sinful culture of their city to be mirrored in their behavior. Jesus describes their spiritual condition as 'lukewarm.'

> "I know your deeds, that you are neither cold nor hot; I wish that you were cold or hot. So because you are lukewarm, and neither hot nor cold, I will spit you out of My mouth."
>
> Revelation 3: 15-16

This analogy of lukewarm water describes a compromised condition. This assembly of believers were not completely dead, but at the same time they were not fully alive. Their lukewarm state places them in flux, they had become indifferent and careless. The consequence for compromise is rejection by Jesus. The actual meaning in the original language is to vomit, which is often seen as vile and violent and associated with severe rejection.

Jesus, when addressing His disciples describes Himself as the true vine and portrays the disciples as the branches. Hundreds of years earlier King

Solomon wrote:

> "Catch the foxes for us, the little foxes that are ruining the vineyards, while our vineyards are in blossom."
>
> Song of Solomon 2:15

We must always be on guard against the little foxes; foxes representing the potential threats to our walk with Jesus. The foxes are little. They are not glaring symbols of compromise, but they represent the real danger of destroying something that is very valuable. Most major falls from grace never happened with a one-time, 180-degree turn from the truth. Similarly, like building success habits, failure happens by small habits compounding together, leading to incremental weakening within your internal foundation until a total breakdown is inevitable.

Do not cooperate with compromise.

Jesus is returning for a group of believers without spot or wrinkle. Paul writes in his letter to the Ephesians:

> "Husbands, love your wives, just as Christ also loved the church and gave Himself up for her, so that He might sanctify her, having cleansed her by the washing of water with the word, that He might present to Himself the church in all her glory, having no spot or wrinkle or any such thing; but that she would be holy and blameless."
>
> Ephesians 5:26-27

The good news is that despite past failures and compromise in your life, God restores. His mercies are new every morning. Isaiah prophesied about Jesus that:

> "…a battered reed He will not break off, and a smoldering wick He will not put out…"
>
> Isaiah 42:3, Matthew 12:20

This is a picture of the Lord breathing life back into those areas where you once were burning for Him. If you are aware of compromise in your life right now, deal with it immediately! Jesus is quick to forgive and restore. He breathes His life into areas where we have fallen and ignites a fire within our life that burns like an all-consuming fire for Him.

COACHING

We must protect ourselves from failure by being aware that we have an enemy and by being aware of our personal failures and weaknesses. Left exposed, these failures and weaknesses carry the potential to derail our mission. We have three enemies we must be aware of and guard against.

SATAN

The Apostle Paul wrote this to the Corinthians: "…so that no advantage would be taken of us by Satan, for we are not ignorant of his schemes" (2 Corinthians 2:11). Jesus also warns us that, "The thief comes to only steal, kill and destroy…" (John 10:10).

OUR FLESH

We must walk uprightly, constantly aware of our own personal struggles with the desires of our flesh. The Apostle Paul wrote, "For the flesh sets its desire against the Spirit, and the Spirit against the flesh; for these are in opposition to one another, so that you may not do the things that you please" (Galatians 5:17).

THE WORLD

Jesus told the disciples in John 16:8 that, "The Holy Spirit will convict the world of sin…" References to the world in Scripture represent the world's systems, which are presently under the influence of the leader of this world (the devil). The Apostle John

COACHING

warns us about the world when he writes, "For all that is in the world, the lust of the flesh and the lust of the eyes and the boastful pride of life, is not from the Father, but is from the world" (1 John 2:16).

We all face temptation. The issue is not whether we will face temptation, but it is how we will react when faced with it. Many honorable and great men have fallen in the faith, because it happens subtly and slowly over time.

At first you may allow yourself to let your glance towards women multiply and turn into a longer stare. Next, you start to cooperate with your physical desire by looking for women who can fill the desire you have started to feed. Next, you may give yourself permission to seek out and proactively look for images and material that is spiritually illegal for you to consume. By aligning your behavior with your thoughts, you have now incrementally moved towards failure. This is how men cheat on their wives. It started with a glance and a thought long before the behavior was engaged in, then it ends in divorce and devastation. This is why Jesus uses strong language when addressing lust. "If your eye causes you to sin, pluck it out."

Book II | Leadership
THE **SHEPHERD'S STAFF**

LEADERSHIP

JESUS IS A SERVANT LEADER

JESUS IS A TEACHER

JESUS IS A COACH

JESUS INVITES US INTO EXPERIENCE

JESUS RESPONDS TO QUESTIONS WITH QUESTIONS

JESUS IS AN ORGANIZATIONAL LEADER

JESUS PRIORITIZES REST

JESUS THE BUSINESSMAN

JESUS REVEALS THE FATHER

"I am the good shepherd; the good shepherd lays down His life for the sheep."

John 10:11

LEADERSHIP

THE GOOD SHEPHERD

Jesus referred to Himself as the Good Shepherd. Why does He use the image of a shepherd? In the times of Jesus, the Galilean hillsides would be filled with sheep and the overseers who were responsible for the flock are known as shepherds. The image Jesus is using would be very familiar to His audience and relays a concept they all can grasp. Jesus presents the shepherd as a picture of leadership. The sheep in this analogy represent the people leaders are called to serve. The shepherd's staff symbolizes strength, authority and protection. In the hand of a leader, it offers safety, security and comfort to those who follow the Shepherd. Jesus is our ultimate role model for leadership. He truly is the Good Shepherd and is described as the shepherd of our souls. We can trust Him.

> "Truly, truly, I say to you, he who does not enter by the door into the fold of the sheep, but climbs up some other way, he is a thief and a robber. But he who enters by the door is a shepherd of the sheep. To him the doorkeeper opens, and the sheep hear his voice, and he calls his own sheep by name and leads them out. When he puts forth all his own, he goes ahead of them, and the sheep follow him because they know his voice. A stranger they simply will not follow, but will flee from him, because they do not know the voice of strangers."
> John 10:1-5

LEADERS USE THE FRONT DOOR

The shepherd enters by the door into the sheepfold. This speaks of proper protocol and order. True leaders institute order and establish protocol and process. Trust is built through clear expectations. Jesus tells us how leaders (shepherds) act and engage when approaching their team (sheep). Entering through the door is a picture of promotion and functioning as the leader.

THE LEADERS VOICE

The sheep hear the leader's voice, he knows them by name and he leads them out. As a leader, he is familiar and accessible to his team, he allows them access and speaks openly with them, sharing secrets and strategies.

THE LEADER KNOWS YOUR NAME

He knows each one by name; this is a picture of being aware of who they are. The leader accounts for their team's strengths, individual personalities and the gift mix they each operate in.

LEADERS LAUNCH LEADERS

He leads them out into their calling, the place of their assignment. "He puts forth all of His own," is translated as waiting for each one to get out into their field at their own pace. He stays behind to ensure all get launched and ensures that no one is left behind. Then he goes ahead and takes the lead. The sheep follow because they know his voice; a voice of authority, instruction and comfort. The sheep love their shepherd's voice, who he is and the way he leads.

LEADERS CREATE LEADERS

As followers of Jesus, we are called to be shepherded and also to become shepherds. Who are your sheep? Who is your team? We are the leaders of our life, so our first qualification is self-leadership. We are also called to be the leaders in our homes and families. Regardless of whether we have a formal leadership title, we are called to be leaders in the workplace and the world. Jesus offers a new paradigm for leadership. In the Kingdom the first is last, the last is first and the way to go up is to go down.

> "But many who are considered to be the most important now will be the least important then. And many who are viewed as the least important now will be considered the most important then."
>
> Mark 10:31 (TPT)

In His Kingdom, leadership is more than being a king – it is being a father. Jesus said, "If you have seen Me, you have seen the Father." As we explore the leadership model Jesus imparts to us, we will see the heart of the Father in protecting, teaching and challenging us. Let's learn from Jesus as we heed the call to assume leadership roles within the Kingdom and sphere of influence God has entrusted to us.

He who has seen Me has seen the Father.
-Jesus
John 14:9

"You know that the rulers of the Gentiles lord it over them, and their great men exercise authority over them. It is not this way among you, but whoever wishes to become great among you shall be your servant, and whoever wishes to be first among you shall be your slave; just as the Son of Man did not come to be served, but to serve, and to give His life a ransom for many."

―――

Matthew 20:25-28

JESUS IS A SERVANT LEADER

What do you think of when you think of leadership? Is your mind flooded with the titles of books you have read, or maybe you have been trained by your employer in the latest leadership model to use in the workplace? Perhaps you think of the best coach you ever played for, the greatest boss you ever worked for or a family member comes to mind. In the Middle East during the times of Jesus the model for leadership were the kings of the day. Jewish Governmental authority and the religious priesthood functioned as the leaders over Israel while being in ultimate submission to the Roman rule of law.

In a private conversation with the twelve disciples, Jesus teaches a new paradigm in which to view leadership. He contrasts the way authority in this world is expressed through the kings of the day and presents a diametrically different model which is rightly referred to as servant leadership (Matthew 20:24-31). The theme of Jesus teaching on leadership is that the first shall be last and the last shall be first (Matthew 19 and 20).

> "…Kings and those with great authority in this world rule oppressively over their subjects, like tyrants. But this is not your calling. You will lead by a completely different model. The greatest one among you will live as the one who is called to serve others, because the greatest honor and authority is reserved for the one with the heart of a servant. For even the Son of Man did not come expecting to be served by everyone, but to serve everyone, and to give his life in exchange for the salvation of many."
>
> Matthew 20:25-28 (TPT)

This is a radical new idea Jesus is introducing – the concept of a servant being greater than a master. Jesus goes beyond stating that servants will be equal to their masters and introduces a concept that shatters the value system of Middle Eastern culture by elevating servants to a place of honor.

SHEEP AND GOATS

On another occasion, Jesus privately addresses His disciples and explains what will happen on judgment day. He states there will be a separation of all nations and people before Him into two groups, which He describes as the sheep on His right side and the goats on His left.

The main qualifiers Jesus references for entrance or denial into His Kingdom are based on how the perceived followers met these needs (Matthew 25:31-46):

- Hungry
- Thirsty
- Homeless
- Poorly clothed
- Sick
- Imprisoned

To the believers who do inherit the Kingdom, He responds:

> "For when you saw me hungry, you fed me. When you found me thirsty, you gave me something to drink. When I had no place to stay, you invited me in, and when I was poorly clothed, you covered me. When I was sick, you tenderly cared for me, and when I was in prison you visited me."
>
> Matthew 25:35-36

These followers display humility in their understanding of their good works and respond to Jesus, "When did we do these things?"

> "And the King will answer them, 'Don't you know? When you cared for one of the least important of these my little ones, my true brothers and sisters, you demonstrated love for me.'"
>
> Matthew 25:40

The group of people referred to as the goats show no awareness of disregarding the King's purposes on that day. Compared to the humility displayed by the sheep, the goats are not mindful that they dishonored the King. This is demonstrated through their line of questioning. "When did we see you in these conditions?"

The King responds:

> "Then he will answer them, 'Don't you know? When you refused to help one of the least important among these my little ones, my true brothers and sisters, you refused to help and honor me.' And they will depart from his presence and go into eternal punishment. But the godly and beloved 'sheep' will enter into eternal bliss."
>
> Matthew 25:45-46 (TPT)

What a striking question: "Don't you know?" By this conversation, we learn that serving others is directly related to honoring the King. The values of the Kingdom are in direct contradiction with the values of this world. The world says climb the ladder, go get yours, by any and all means possible and be first. Serving others is the highest expression of the values of leadership in God's Kingdom.

> "But many who push themselves to be first will find themselves last. And those who are willing to be last will find themselves to be first."
> **-Jesus**
> Matthew 19:30 (TPT)

The Kingdom of God is in opposition to this world, its systems and way of thinking. Jesus the Christ, God who humbled Himself and became a man, lived a life marked by self-sacrifice and humility. At His last meal with His disciples, Jesus does something unthinkable for all those at the table with Him. He kneels down, only this time He is not kneeling down in prayer. He is kneeling down in a public display before His followers as the ultimate servant. One by one He takes their feet and washes them. He serves them in an act that will forever be memorialized.

Can you see the Lord of all the earth as He takes the lowest position as a servant, washing the dirt, grime and dust from the disciples' weathered feet? The highest office and title in the Kingdom of God is marked by how well you serve, honor and love others. This is true leadership… servant leadership.

COACHING

Many aspire to leadership positions for the honor that comes with the title, the pride of updating their resume and social media profiles and the perks that go along with the new position. That is not the leadership that Jesus models. All men are leaders. You are called to be a leader in your world and should dedicate and develop yourself towards opportunities that allow you to lead others. Formal leadership positions are not something to shy away from, embrace them, as they provide the perfect opportunity to serve the people who report to you.

I have been privileged to hold formal leadership positions managing teams of people and had the opportunity to demonstrate servant leadership that truly serves and honors others. I've been able to produce generational impact because those I've been responsible for have gone on to mentor, inspire and serve others who they lead differently. The DNA of a leader is duplication: leaders create more leaders. We are called to carry and bring God's Kingdom everywhere we go, creating a new culture. Honoring everyone around you shifts the atmosphere and helps align those you serve with their purpose, unlocks their potential and allows them to align with their calling.

"When Jesus saw the crowds, He went up on the mountain; and after He sat down, His disciples came to Him. He opened His mouth and began to teach them…"

Matthew 5:1-2

JESUS IS A TEACHER

One of the most common titles others labeled Jesus with during His ministry was 'Rabbi' – the translation is master teacher. Jesus carried an authority and confidence in the truths He taught, and this was recognized by the unschooled as well as the religiously-educated elite.

> "The people were awestruck and overwhelmed by his teaching, because he taught in a way that demonstrated God's authority, which was quite unlike the religious scholars."
>
> Mark 1:22 (TPT)

Jesus was disruptive in the way He presented heavenly realities. He spoke in the common language of the day and painted detailed word pictures that were stunningly sharp and could be understood by all.

> "Become like a child" (Mark 9:36)

> "Love Your neighbor as yourself" (Mark 12:31)

He also used metaphors and hyperbole to create powerful images to drive the point home.

> "If your hand causes you to sin, cut it off" (Matthew 18:8)

> "If your eye causes you to sin, pluck it out" (Matthew 18:9)

These are not literal directions to dismember your physical body, but they are vivid images that represent the severity and weight of sin's effect. The point here is to literally cut sin off. These teaching moments would also include straightforward explanations of a truth or principle with no ambiguity.

One of the key themes in the teachings of Jesus is that we must remain teachable. In Matthew 18, He instructs all listening to become teachable like little children. Jesus coaches, corrects and also teaches. He captures teachable moments constantly with His disciples, consistently demonstrating to them that they must remain teachable. It is more than just having the mindset of a student; it is an attitude of the heart.

> "Listen to the truth I speak: Whoever does not open their arms to receive God's kingdom like a teachable child will never enter it."
>
> Mark 10:15

Immediately following this statement from Jesus in Mark's Gospel, we can read the famous account of the rich young ruler, a wealthy man who approaches Jesus addressing Him as 'Good Teacher.' The story unfolds and we quickly learn that calling Jesus 'teacher' is not the same as being teachable.

Have you ever got an opportunity where you dropped the ball? Something you wish you could get a 'do-over' on? This man gets a moment with Jesus and has no idea that his words will live within the pages of the Bible for future generations to learn from. He was not prepared for his opportunity and missed the moment to step into the invitation of Jesus. The scene unfolds before us with Jesus preparing to depart for His next destination. Picture Jesus as He goes out into the road and a man runs towards Him, falls down before Him and begins to praise Him as 'good teacher.' Jesus engages the man in a dialogue, peeling back the layers of this young man's heart in an attempt to lead him to the truth. The young man recounts all of his good effort in keeping the commandments of Moses.

> "Jesus fixed his gaze upon the man, with tender love, and said to him, 'Yet there is still one thing in you lacking. Go, sell all that you have and give the money to the poor. Then all of your treasure will be in heaven. After you've done this, come back and walk with me.'"
>
> Mark 10:21 (TPT)

There were many encounters recorded in the gospels where the person impacted or healed by Jesus asked permission to follow Him. Numerous times Jesus gave instruction to either return to your village, go and show yourself to the priests or stay here and share your testimony. It was rarer to find an exclusive invitation to "Come and follow me," which literally translates to come and walk with me on the same road. Jesus requests that this young man sell everything he has to join Him. This is not a universal command to anyone who accumulates wealth, nor is it a conversation about stewarding our material possessions and investments. In every interaction, Jesus customized His teaching to the individual. He knew this man's heart and that this man did not just possess riches, but the riches possessed him.

Calling Jesus teacher is not the same as being teachable

It is easy for us to armchair quarterback this and claim that we would never make such a foolish decision. However, we do not know what lies within our own heart until we are standing in that place and in that moment. Imagine how this man's life's story could have been different. Perhaps he would become a notable follower of Jesus. Maybe we would have learned his name and what he accomplished within the Kingdom of God as a first-century disciple or missionary. When presented the opportunity of his lifetime, he could not accept the invitation because he did not allow himself to be teachable by the 'Good Teacher.'

COACHING

The day you stop being teachable is the day you stop learning. Everything in God's Kingdom is progressive, always moving and advancing us to the next level. This means we are to always be developing spiritually, and one of the ways we learn is from teaching. God uses men and women in our life to teach us His ways. Sometimes these teachings will be direct, and other times we learn from what we observe and are modeled. At times we will also learn what not to do. I strive to keep the mindset that I can learn from anyone, whether they are a CEO of a large organization or they clean the floors in that organization. I believe all of us have things we can learn and also things we can teach. Ultimately the Holy Spirit is our teacher and He will lead us into all truth. So, when you're going through a hard lesson in life, ask Holy Spirit what He is teaching you.

> But the Helper, the Holy Spirit, whom the Father will send in My name, He will teach you all things, and bring to your remembrance all that I said to you.
>
> John 14:26

"But He said to them, 'You give them something to eat!'"

Luke 9:13

JESUS IS A COACH

What comes to mind when you think of a coach?

- Someone who challenges you?
- Someone who stretches you beyond your normal capacity?
- Someone who requires more of you than you would normally require of yourself?

Yes, coaches do all of the above and more. The goal of a coaching, whether in sport or industry, is to develop you into your full potential. That is God's heart for us – that we would obtain all that is available to us through Him and live our lives in the fullness of what Christ paid for on the cross. Jesus calls this the abundant life.

> "…I have come so that they may have life, and may have it abundantly."
>
> John 10:10b

The word abundant here refers to more than we would expect or anticipate, a life that offers us advantage and more than what is necessary.

Jesus is the master coach. He challenges us to become more – to give our all and do something, so we can become what we are called to be and walk in all we are to have. He takes us beyond what we thought possible of ourselves. The Bible has a long history of God using ordinary people to do great things for Him and shape history, that in and of themselves they would not be able to accomplish. Think of David – the shepherd boy who was the least of his brothers and overlooked by his own father, Jesse. When Samuel the prophet asked to meet Jesse's sons, David wasn't even included in the lineup. They had to go and get David from the field because Samuel wanted to see him and his father had overlooked him. This ruddy shepherd boy defeated an enemy giant, was promoted to be king of the nation of Israel, led armies in conquest and started the temple's building process.

JESUS COACHES TO INCREASE OUR CAPACITY

Jesus places a demand on us to challenge and stretch us to our full capacity. We witness an example of this in the following New Testament account found in Luke chapter 9 (9:13-17). One day when Jesus is teaching in the Galilean countryside, 5,000 people gathered and camped around Him to listen to His message. As the day ended, the disciples (who are most likely feeling pressure and are under some anxiety to facilitate the logistics of this gathering) approach Jesus and ask Him to send the crowds away for food and lodging. The answer they receive is not what they were expecting. Jesus emphatically responds, "You give them something to eat." There was an emotional command and urgency in His voice found in the original language.

The disciples object by responding that the only food they have with them is five loaves of bread and two fish. Jesus challenges them and uses a coaching process to stretch His team and take them to the next level. He leads the way and instructs His disciples to organize the people into groups. He blesses and breaks the bread and hands it out to the disciples to distribute until everyone is fed. When the meal is finished, they end up with 12 baskets full of left overs.

Five loaves and two fish fed 5,000 people (potentially 10,000 people when you account for women and children), plus generated 12 baskets of leftovers. Coaching is different than teaching. When Jesus acts as coach, some lessons are not transferred with words. There were things the disciples had to 'catch' from these experiences. Let's take a closer look at five lessons wrapped within this experience of the feeding of the 5,000.

1. FOCUS ON WHAT YOU HAVE

When problems and challenges arise, our natural minds and logic tend to immediately focus on what we do not have. It is far easier to justify why you cannot do something, why you are not ready or do not have what's needed. Jesus takes what's in their hand and multiplies it. What's in your hand today? Start with a focus on what you have and not on what you do not have.

2. SEE WITH EYES OF FAITH

Jesus takes us into the impossible, because He sees what others do not see. He stretches us and always speaks the language of faith. Jesus operates out of the spiritual realm to see the miracle, but seeing it also affects the natural mind and outlook in every situation. I am confident that if you hang out with Jesus long enough, like the disciples did, you will start to re-wire your brain to see things that others do not. Jesus always sees you and speaks to you from your future and what you are called to be.

3. DO NOT FEAR AND DOUBT

It is normal to look at natural circumstances in life and rationalize everything to the point of never moving forward in the areas of your assignment. Fear and doubt do not immediately disappear the moment you put your faith in God's plan for you. There is a decision we each need to make to step forward despite how we 'feel.' In this situation, the disciples were mentored into the miracle, but the day will be coming when they will be doing mighty works on their own without the physical presence of their mentor. Jesus prepares them for that coming day.

4. TRUST HIM

Taking action and moving forward in what we are called to do is not rooted in self-generated will power. I love this multiplication miracle, because even as the miracle is unfolding, we have a picture of the disciples meeting needs by their hands, literally handing out food to the people. However, Jesus is the source. The Bible says, "He broke off pieces of bread and fish and kept giving more to each disciple to give to the crowd." The pressure is not on us to perform; Jesus is supplying what we need as we step out. When Jesus calls you to do something, He always equips you with resources to accomplish the assignment.

5. EMPLOY A POSITIVE KINGDOM OUTLOOK

Jesus is the ultimate optimist, but not as the world understands optimism. His outlook comes from complete trust and reliance upon His Father. A very impactful form of coaching is 'modeling.' In this miracle, Jesus is modeling the behavior of the Kingdom. He is operating in a manner that He will soon expect the disciples to operate in when He is no longer physically present with them. He is teaching them to think like He does, see the need and believe God to meet it. Step out by taking an action and put your total trust in your Father to fulfill what He has asked you to. Jesus sees us from our future and coaches us to see ourselves from our future as well.

COACHING

I am a strong believer in coaching, I have had the opportunity to serve others in the role of coach and have greatly benefited from receiving coaching. Regardless of your status, title or position, everyone needs a coach – even coaches need coaches! There is a reason some of the greatest athletes on earth have coaches. My goal for myself and my desire for you is that you would reach your full potential in all areas of your life. It would be a sad day if we were ever shown what we 'could' have accomplished, but didn't because we never reached our full capacity.

Abundant life in every area is my goal, including my walk with Jesus, my relationship with my wife and family, in business, health, and finances. If your view of the Christian life does not encompass an abundance mentality in all of these areas, elevate your perspective of God and His goodness. This is how I walk in the overflow of superabundance in my relationship with the Lord.

"Beloved friend, I pray that you are prospering in every way and that you continually enjoy good health, just as your soul is prospering."

3 John 1:2 (TPT)

"And He said, 'Come!' And Peter got out of the boat, and walked on the water and came toward Jesus."

Matthew 14:29

JESUS INVITES US INTO EXPERIENCE

The Eastern mindset values experiential learning contrasted to the didactic style of the Western world's classrooms. Jesus teaches, models and invites us into experience and challenges us to grow. Recent studies have shown that having an experience with the subject matter is the ultimate standard for learning, helping our brains gain neuroplasticity, retain and utilize what we learn. Matthew documents the account when Peter and the other disciples were in a boat during a storm, crossing the sea of Galilee. Jesus appears to them a distance away, walking on the water.

> "And in the fourth watch of the night He came to them, walking on the sea. When the disciples saw Him walking on the sea, they were terrified, and said, "It is a ghost!" And they cried out in fear. But immediately Jesus spoke to them, saying, "'Take courage, it is I; do not be afraid.' Peter said to Him, 'Lord, if it is You, command me to come to You on the water.' And He said, 'Come!' And Peter got out of the boat, and walked on the water and came toward Jesus."
>
> Matthew 14:25-29

In this experience, Jesus does something that required faith to believe. By appearing in this manner, He is demonstrating that He is not limited to the earth and its natural laws. He is modeling something that defies everything they have ever known. It offends logic and cannot be received by the natural mind. This very act was an invitation into discovery. It stirs the men to extreme curiosity, until Peter asks for an invitation to join in.

This is how a student who is ready to learn responds. Jesus challenges Peter to exercise His faith and step out of the boat. Jesus does not go into the boat or take Peter by the hand and escort him onto the water. He invites Peter and waits. Peter is the one who must decide and take the first step. Jesus does not move Peter's legs for him, but He does support and uphold him as he walks forward in faith.

Many times, we are waiting on God to do 'the thing' for us, whatever it may be. Jesus' will for us is that we are changed and grow into full maturity. Sometimes He may provide the answer, radically change our situation and intervene. All things are possible. However, the higher way, the way Jesus taught, the way He modelled and instructed is that we would act as kings under His headship. He can move the mountain Himself, but as He told His disciples:

"If you have faith, YOU can move the mountain."

When you become a believer and follower of Jesus, the very act of deciding to follow Him opens the gateway to experience. He draws us to Himself and invites us into participation within His Kingdom. When Jesus first calls the disciples to Himself, there is a formal installation and transference of His authority and power.

> "And He went up on the mountain and summoned those whom He Himself wanted, and they came to Him. And He appointed twelve, so that they would be with Him and that He could send them out to preach, and to have authority to cast out the demons."
>
> Mark 3:13-15

The first invitation into experience is the invitation to simply be with Him. This is true discipleship, walking the same road, being taught by the Lord and learning His ways. This is the invitation into participation, fellowship and friendship we receive when we first meet Him. The next agreement Jesus makes with us is an impartation to carry His authority for the purpose of sending. He empowers us as partners to carry His Kingdom and destroy the works of darkness wherever we go. The Apostle John will later write about this purpose of Jesus:

> "The Son of God appeared for this purpose, to destroy the works of the devil."
>
> 1 John 3:8b

COACHING

THE FIVE AGREEMENTS

The five agreements Jesus has with the disciples as He calls them to the top of the mountain (Mark 3:13-15).

1. HE CALLS US HIGHER

"Jesus went up on a mountainside and called to himself the men he wanted to be his close companions, so they went up the mountainside to join him."

Everything Jesus does is purposeful and intentional. There are no coincidences or casual occurrences with the way He operates. He summons the disciples to the mountain top. Brothers, He is calling us to the mountain top as well. Jesus invites us to come up higher. He wants us to elevate our view of who He is, who we are and of our surroundings. This is the first agreement Jesus brings us into, as we summit the mountaintop to meet Him.

2. HE DESTINES US

"…He appointed the Twelve…"

He calls us, then appoints. Brian Simmons in The Passion Translation points out that, "This was not simply a passive acknowledgment, but an active setting them in place. The Greek verb poieo is the verb 'do' or 'make.' Jesus 'did' them; that is, he imparted his favor, blessing, and grace to set them in place as apostolic emissaries for the kingdom realm of God" (TPT Note E, Mark 3:14).

Jesus sets us in place, provides our assignment and imparts the

COACHING

grace we need to carry our mission and run our course.

3. HE WANTS US TO BE WITH HIM

"…whom he named apostles. He wanted them to be continually at his side as his friends…"

Everything in the Kingdom is relational and about family. Jesus desires relationship and that His friends would abide with Him. This is the same for you and I. He is not looking for just 'workers,' so He adopts us into the family as heirs and desires for us to walk with Him.

4. HE SEND US OUT ON ASSIGNMENT

"…so that he could send them out to preach…"

After relationship is established, there is a 'sending.' Each of us is called to carry the message of the Kingdom into the sphere of influence we are called to. We are called to witness with our actions and our words.

5. EMPOWERED WITH AUTHORITY

"…and have authority to heal the sick and to cast out demons."

Jesus empowers and equips those He calls with His authority. He sends us out as emissaries and ambassadors of His Kingdom. We are representatives, and as such we have the full backing of heaven to accomplish all He has called us to do. We are to bring the battle to the enemy's territory, because as spiritual warriors, we are called to fight.

"And a lawyer stood up and put Him to the test, saying, "Teacher, what shall I do to inherit eternal life?" And He said to him, "What is written in the Law? How does it read to you?"

Luke 10:25-26

JESUS RESPONDS TO QUESTIONS WITH QUESTIONS

Questions are extremely powerful. Questions are great tools in higher learning used to dig deep and facilitate an understanding of a subject. In relationship dynamics, questions are incredibly useful to frame context, facilitate trust and understand others' points of view. They also serve as evidence of deeper thought, genuine interest and critical thinking. Jesus uses questions consistently in His ministry. In the Bible, He asks 300+ questions to accomplish all of the above and more.

It is common to see Jesus respond to a question with a question. He does this to provoke thought, invoke curiosity and lead those He engages with into the truth. The verse above is a great example of how Jesus poses questions to those who engage with Him. Interestingly, Jesus does not answer all questions asked of Him. In fact, when He responds to a question with a question, His reply is usually predicated with how the person answers His question. Matthew records an example of such an occurrence. Here, Jesus has an interaction with the Pharisees and beautifully uses one powerful question to navigate this interaction.

> "When He entered the temple, the chief priests and the elders of the people came to Him while He was teaching, and said, 'By what authority are You doing these things, and who gave You this authority?' Jesus said to them, 'I will also ask you one thing, which if you tell Me, I will also tell you by what authority I do these things. The baptism of John was from what source, from heaven or from men?' And they began reasoning among themselves, saying, 'If we say, 'From heaven,' He will say to us, 'Then why did you not believe him?' But if we say, 'From men,' we fear the people; for they all regard John as a prophet.' And answering Jesus, they said, 'We do not know.' He also said to them, 'Neither will I tell you by what authority I do these things.'"
>
> Matt 21:23-27

The Pharisees ask a powerful question and seek to challenge and ensnare Jesus. Jesus responds to the Pharisees with a question that challenges and places the burden of responsibility and accountability on them in front of all present. He never let them have an inch of control in this interaction. He maintains power in this engagement. To respond to someone's question is a shift of power within an interaction. He turns the tables on His challengers by not answering and taking the power of the interaction back with His question. When they cannot answer, He does not feel the need to submit to their request. He emerges as the victor of this interaction as well as never giving away His power position.

Jesus does not only use questions to those who challenge Him, He also uses questions with His team throughout their discipling process. The most effective tool used in coaching are questions. Jesus uses many types of questions to cause the hearer to lean in and awaken their curiosity.

- "Have I been with you for so long a time and you still do not know me?"
- "Why do you not understand what I am saying?"
- "You of little faith, why did you doubt?"

JESUS DOES NOT ALWAYS PROVIDE THE ANSWER

The best coaches do not provide the answer directly. Why? To do so is to undermine learning and bypass inspiring contemplation. The greatest coaches and teachers provide the atmosphere and environment where learning can be facilitated. This type of coaching process leads the learner into truth by instilling the desire to search out and go deeper into the subject at hand. Jesus leads you to the truth through your learning process.

One day when speaking with His disciples, Jesus confirmed that Elijah must come first.

"And His disciples asked Him, 'Why then do the scribes say that

Elijah must come first?' And He answered and said, 'Elijah is coming and will restore all things; but I say to you that Elijah already came, and they did not recognize him, but did to him whatever they wished. So also the Son of Man is going to suffer at their hands.' Then the disciples understood that He had spoken to them about John the Baptist."

Matt 17:10-13

Notice Jesus never explicitly shares with His disciples that John the Baptist was who He was referring to. Instead He says enough to lead them to connect the dots on their own. This is the method of the Master.

- Questions provoke thought
- Questions inspire the search
- Questions cause deep reflection

There is no reason to believe that Jesus does not still use questions today. Many times, when you are spending time with the Lord, He desires that you ask Him about the questions you are facing, this is a great way to engage Jesus in your devotional time. Expect to not always receive the answer you seek in a direct word. Be prepared to dialogue with your Lord as He draws you deeper into relationship with Him.

Questions accomplish what providing the answer cannot do.

COACHING

Men should build trust in all of their interactions. This life skill will serve you well as you progress through your career, your daily interactions and in building relationships. Genuine interest is a hallmark of the Kingdom. Jesus says we will be known by our love. One of the ways we exhibit love in our daily interactions is by asking questions; asking because we genuinely care. One practical way to display deep listening skills is to be more interested than interesting. Can you imagine how those around you would feel if you started demonstrating light by taking an interest in their personal situation? Start today by bypassing superficial talking points and go deeper by asking thoughtful questions to those who cross your path. I believe there are new relationships and connections waiting for us if we take the time to invest our attention into developing them.

"Then he instructed them to organize the crowd and have them sit down in groups on the grass. So they had them sit down in groups of hundreds and fifties."

Mark 6:39-40

JESUS IS AN ORGANIZATIONAL LEADER

Jesus showed up on the scene in a small town in Israel over 2,000 years ago. There were no modern technologies to help Him spread His message; no newspapers, television or social media. There were no advertising courses or studies to prove what is the best method for marketing your message. Despite this, Jesus impacts the earth in such a way to split the calendar system in two and launch the biggest movement in earth's history from this small corner of the globe. There were no church buildings, membership or perks to offer converts. Quite the contrary…becoming Christ's follower in the first century was almost a guarantee for persecution and even death.

Great leaders institute order. Jesus brings order to chaos, and not only in the spiritual sense. Organization is something exhibited throughout His life on earth. For example, Jesus chooses a team of 12 men. He had a treasurer, which tells us He had enough financial resources to necessitate one. It also demonstrates they set up an organized financial process for how the money was received and filtered to meet the needs of Jesus, His disciples and the poor.

HE DELEGATES AND DUPLICATES

Within the team of 12, there are three who comprise His inner circle. In Mark chapter six (Mark 6:7-13, Matthew 10), during His first year of ministry, Jesus sends out the 12 in pairs on their first missionary journey. In addition to the 12, we see that Jesus has other followers – those who walked with Him from town to town. These are men and women who have received His message, although they are not part of the core team. In Luke chapter 10, Jesus addresses 70 others who have been following Him, learning His ways and received an impartation of His power. He organizes these 70 (in addition to His disciples) into 35 groups of two and sends them forth with clear expectations and directions.

INSPECT WHAT YOU EXPECT

Great leaders set clear expectations. Almost all issues we face with our relationships at home and work can be attributed to a breakdown in communication. When expectations are not clearly communicated, people are left to interpret the goal on their own. No progress can be made if there are not clear milestones and metrics of how the mission will be measured, and at times we may have expectations others have not agreed to.

Jesus gave clear direction to the teams, and you can read more details in Luke 10:1-16. He empowers and trains them for the mission, He sets clear goals, provides them with the script and demonstrates how to respond to those they are traveling to. He prepares them by addressing their practical needs, such as food and finances, and coaching them on the potential encounters they may have.

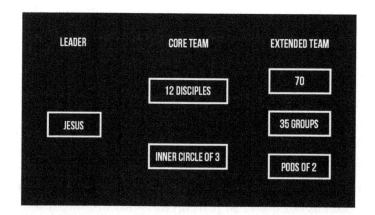

When you look at this visual, you can see the strategy behind His system. We can observe that Jesus never isolates one disciple for a mission – His preferred environment for ministry and mission is accomplished within a team.

There are benefits to partnering. There is a power of multiplication within God's Kingdom. Consider the following instructions given to the nation of Israel through Moses:

> "How could one chase a thousand, and two put ten thousand to flight, unless their Rock had sold them, and the Lord had given them up?"
>
> Deuteronomy 32:30

When Israel obeyed God and partnered with Him, the effects of their numbers and partnerships are compounded through the force multiplication of God.

> "But you will chase your enemies and they will fall before you by the sword; five of you will chase a hundred, and a hundred of you will chase ten thousand, and your enemies will fall before you by the sword."
>
> Leviticus 26:7-8

5 will chase 100
100 will chase 10,000

Wisdom is found in going together, and the effects of combined efforts produces magnified results

The principle behind this pattern is this: there is an increase that comes through working together, beyond what we could accomplish on our own. King Solomon wrote, "Iron sharpens iron, so one man sharpens another" (Proverbs 27:17). The wise king also wrote:

> "Two are better than one because they have a good return for their labor. For if either of them falls, the one will lift up his companion. But woe to the one who falls when there is not another to lift him up.

> Furthermore, if two lie down together they keep warm, but how can one be warm alone? And if one can overpower him who is alone, two can resist him. A cord of three strands is not quickly torn apart."
>
> Ecclesiastes 4:9-12

Wisdom is found in going together, and the effects of combined efforts produces magnified results. There are clear instructions from the writer of Hebrews to the early church that they are not to stop meeting together. We must always be aware of our enemy and his tactics. He roams like a lion, seeking to devour prey. Strength comes in numbers and one of the strategies he employs is isolation. God's answer to the enemy's plan is community. Jesus came to set up a Kingdom that is not of this world. This Kingdom is more akin to a colony than an organization. Because we are a living temple, we are better compared to a living organism than a man-made organization. Jesus institutes protocol, order and organization within His Kingdom.

COACHING

BATTLE BORN

A word on isolation: many men think they can survive on their own. This is a lie of the enemy and is a proven way to set yourself up for failure and frustration. As born-again believers, when we enter the Kingdom we are born into battle. Jesus was explicit in His message that the Kingdom suffers violence and the violent take it by force. Make no mistake. We are in a war, and you will not thrive if you attempt to walk alone. Collateral damage and casualties await those who are isolated. We have observed in the Kingdom the instruction to band together. Men need brothers who they can fight with.

God's multiplication of combined efforts happens when more than one person gathers. The spiritual synergy truly ignites when two or more like-minded brothers come together in unity. You need to travel with a tribe that is marching towards the same goal. Isolation is not the answer and two are better than one.

"When the apostles returned, they gave an account to Him of all that they had done. Taking them with Him, He withdrew by Himself to a city called Bethsaida."

Luke 9:10

JESUS PRIORITIZES REST

As a leader, Jesus is concerned with the care of His team. He is their spiritual leader, imparting the ways of the Kingdom, explaining deeper revelation and spiritual truth. At the same time, He is extremely practical and concerned with not only their spiritual needs, but also their natural needs. He understands and demonstrates the principle of rest, as rest is important because it creates endurance to fulfill their calling. His life was marked by serving, working and moving among the crowds for many full days of ministry. This work would have been physically taxing as people pull on Him, make requests and gather everywhere He goes to hear Him teach. After ministry days like this, there is a definite need for rest to endure the physical stress His mission would place on Him and His team.

Consider what Jesus did in one snapshot of His ministry recorded in Mark chapters 4 and 5. The scene starts in Mark chapter 4. Jesus is teaching the people, and when He is done, He sends the crowds away, but they attempt to follow Him and the disciples. As He travels across the lake, a fierce storm arises and Jesus speaks peace to it. Upon arriving at shore, Jesus will set a demon-possessed man free. Afterwards, He travels back across the lake, and as soon as He and the disciples land on shore, a man named Jairus pushes his way through the crowd to make a request of Jesus. His daughter is very ill and he seeks the attention of Jesus. Jesus agrees and follows Jairus to his home. On the way, a random woman will touch Jesus' garment and be healed, causing Jesus to stop on the road and ask who touched Him. The disciples respond, "What do you mean? The crowds are huge and everyone is pressing up against you." Jesus takes the time to minister to the woman who touched Him. He will continue on to raise the daughter of Jairus from the dead, despite the unbelief and naysayers, and He will do all these things in front of a crowd comprised of earnest seekers, skeptical onlookers and the gaze of the religiously proud.

These circumstances will also prove to be testing for the disciples. These 12 men literally transitioned from obscurity to the center stage of their day. The disciples are thrust into the middle of ministry, and the peaceful life many of them knew before will never be the same again.

Jesus will equip, empower and send out the 12 on their first ministry journey. He celebrates them upon their return and prioritizes a time of rest and recovery.

> "The apostles returned from their mission and gathered around Jesus and told him everything they had done and taught. There was such a swirl of activity around Jesus, with so many people coming and going, that they were unable to even eat a meal. So Jesus said to his disciples, 'Come, let's take a break and find a secluded place where you can rest a while.' They slipped away and left by sailboat for a deserted spot."
> Mark 6:30-31 (TPT)

Jesus served His team after they ministered. We see Jesus caring for the disciples in a practical way. His men need nutrition, His men need rest and His men need some private time to debrief and be among themselves. There is a time for ministry and there is a time for rest.

> "When the apostles returned, they gave an account to Him of all that they had done. Taking them with Him, He withdrew by Himself to a city called Bethsaida."
> Luke 9:10

Luke records that Jesus 'withdrew.' The life of Jesus is marked by giving. Living in a physical body will require downtime and time spent recharging. To work at full capacity requires intervals: there is a time to work and a time to rest. In order to fulfill your assignment, Jesus models that rest is necessary. Rest makes us more effective – we are able to give out more because we took the time for self-care. Jesus recharges through His prayer life and time spent in solitude with His Father, as well as time with His friends.

We also get insight into the important balance Jesus places on the physical upkeep of not only Himself but His followers. Jesus was no doubt in good physical shape based on His time spent as a builder, His activity level and the Middle-Eastern diet He would have been accustomed to. Through His actions with His disciples, He gives His followers a 'rest' model to follow. They are learning through observation how to treat themselves and also how to teach balance to the followers they will have later in their lives.

JESUS HAS A SABBATH

We see the principle of rest in Genesis chapter 2 when God rested. The Sabbath (day of rest) was instituted by God in the Old Testament, and we see that Jesus also honors a day of rest in His life.

> "One Saturday, on the day of rest, Jesus and his disciples were walking through a field of wheat. The disciples were hungry, so they plucked off some heads of grain and rubbed them in their hands to eat."
>
> Matt 12:1 (TPT)

In the following interaction with the religious order, Jesus states;

> "For the Son of Man is Lord of the Sabbath."
> Matthew 12:8

COACHING

THE IMPORTANCE OF REST

Life in the 21st Century is quite different and more complex than first century living. If rest is a priority for Jesus and His disciples, how much more should we as modern men prioritize a time of rest to recharge and restore our stamina? The fact of the matter is that if I am not keeping up with the physical, emotional and mental demands of my day, I am not functioning at full capacity and not maximizing my impact. Sometimes we need to take one step back to take three steps forward. Every athlete knows the importance of rest and recovery time in a training program as they are building strength, power and endurance. In training, muscle growth is facilitated when you are in a state of rest. We, too, must prioritize rest and maintain a 'day of rest' to conquer life and take dominion over what we are called to subdue.

"And he called ten of his slaves, and gave them ten minas and said to them, 'Do business with this until I come back.'"

Luke 19:13

JESUS IS A BUSINESSMAN

An often-overlooked attribute of God as described by Jesus is that of entrepreneur and business owner. One of the major cornerstones to the economy of Israel at the time period of Jesus was agriculture. Jesus spoke in common language, using metaphors His listeners would understand as part of their ordinary dialogue. It would be easy for the Eastern mindset to grasp word pictures describing farming, planting and reaping, work in vineyards and other agricultural metaphors.

Farmers in this time period were the entrepreneurs, business owners and the sole proprietors of their day. They would be responsible for the business strategy, operations, execution, marketing, sales, forecasting, managing of budgets, employees, and most of all ensuring they have a plan in place for profitability.

Through the use of parables, we see another side of the Lord's character: Jesus the business man, the manager and owner. Let's take a closer look at the business side of God.

In Matthew chapter 13, Jesus teaches in many parables. Below are five parables where He depicts Himself in the role of business owner.

IN THE PARABLE OF THE SEED / SOIL

Jesus is the farmer who sows seed. The climactic moment in this story is the harvest, when the proprietor reaps a return on His investment at 30, 60 and 100-fold above the original investment.

IN THE PARABLE OF THE WEEDS
Jesus, self-described as the Son of Man in the parable, is the farmer who sows and owns the field. He makes wise and prudent decisions to preserve the integrity of His crop. He is concerned with the harvest and the return on His investment

IN THE PARABLE OF THE HIDDEN TREASURE
Jesus is the investor who purchases the field so He can have the treasure. He invests in the field for the purpose of making a return on His investment.

IN THE PARABLE OF THE COSTLY PEARL
Jesus is the merchant in search of rare pearls with high value.

IN THE PARABLE OF THE FISHING NET
Jesus is the master fisherman who owns the boat, the net and is in control of the catch, gathering the good fish into containers and discarding the bad fish.

One of the themes that I have underscored with the role Jesus illustrates in all of these parables is Jesus as businessman or investor that is actively seeking a return on His investment (ROI).

In the Parable of the Minas found in Luke 19:11-27, Jesus tells a story of a nobleman who departs on a journey and calls ten servants and provided them with ten minas each (a mina is equal to around 100 day's wages). When the king returns, he calls each servant to collect the return on his investment.

- The first servant has taken the one mina and made an additional ten minas. As a reward, the servant is given authority over ten cities.

- The second servant has taken the one mina and made an additional five minas. As a reward, this servant is given authority over five cities.

Another servant returned the one mina he had been entrusted with, giving the following explanation:

> "…for I was afraid of you, because you are an exacting man; you take up what you did not lay down and reap what you did not sow.'

The master responds bluntly to this servant:

> "He said to him, 'By your own words I will judge you, you worthless slave. Did you know that I am an exacting man, taking up what I did not lay down and reaping what I did not sow? Then why did you not put my money in the bank, and having come, I would have collected it with interest?' Then he said to the bystanders, 'Take the mina away from him and give it to the one who has the ten minas.' And they said to him, 'Master, he has ten minas already.' I tell you that to everyone who has, more shall be given, but from the one who does not have, even what he does have shall be taken away. But these enemies of mine, who did not want me to reign over them, bring them here and slay them in my presence."
>
> Luke 19:22-27

JESUS HOLDS US ACCOUNTABLE

Jesus makes an investment and then demands the ROI. There is a business side of God where He will one day hold us all accountable for what we did with what we have.

SALVATION IS FREE

Salvation is a gift that was purchased through the shed blood of Jesus Christ. We receive this free gift through grace and faith. There is nothing we can do of our own works to earn, merit or work for our salvation (Ephesians 2:8).

AFTER SALVATION

It is clear in Scripture that there will be a judgement of those who believe, with crowns and rewards given. Not all believers produce a return on investment and not all will attain the prize. The Apostle Paul writes of two different kinds of building materials used, spiritually.

> "Now if any man builds on the foundation with gold, silver, precious stones, wood, hay, straw, each man's work will become evident; for the day will show it because it is to be revealed with fire, and the fire itself will test the quality of each man's work. If any man's work which he has built on it remains, he will receive a reward. If any man's work is burned up, he will suffer loss; but he himself will be saved, yet so as through fire."
>
> 1 Corinthians 3:12-15

COACHING

Are you aware of what God has called you to? You do not need to see the whole picture of your life's calling and ultimate purpose to start moving in the direction of His call for you today. I believe the Lord has placed God dreams, vision and aspirations within your heart and in your hand. What is the thing you want to accomplish? What brings you the most fulfillment? Has God personally spoken to you or inspired you through a dream or vision of what you are to accomplish for Him?

A few years ago, I heard the Lord speak to me and say:

> "I want a return on My investment."

I immediately knew He was speaking to me about the deposits He has made in my life and how there will be a day when I will be evaluated and held accountable for what I did with what I had. This caused me to take inventory of all the valuable blessings I have in my life – things like my spiritual and natural giftings, relationships, trainings I have received and skills I have acquired.

The Lord deposits valuable treasure in each of us. Then, it is our responsibility to develop and steward the treasures He has placed within and around us. The treasure is not limited to the following, but can reveal itself as:

- Spiritual truths that are revealed to you
- Divine connections and relationships
- Natural skills and abilities
- Spiritual gifts that are given to edify and build up others
- Motivational and encouraging gifts
- Physical and material means and resources that can be used for His glory

COACHING

I believe you have abilities, skills, talents and wisdom within certain areas of your life. My hope is that this book gives you a strong foundation in your understanding of God's nature and purpose for you; a foundation upon which you discover, develop and learn to walk in the calling and assignments He has for you.

"...He who has seen Me has seen the Father."

John 14:9

JESUS REVEALS THE FATHER

What was your experience like with your father? Whether you had a great experience with your earthly father or he didn't meet your expectations, you have a Heavenly Father who loves you. There is an attack on the family, and most of the declining stats within our society can be traced back to fatherlessness. According to the U.S. Census Bureau, 19.7 million children, more than 1 in 4, live without a father in the home. (2017. U.S. Census Bureau. Data represent children living without a biological, step, or adoptive father.)

We witness the casualties this attack has created for us as a society. Thankfully, Jesus gives us a model for how to relate to our Heavenly Father and demonstrates the Father in a tangible way. Jesus brings a healthy Father/Son relationship into focus, past the stigmas we may have assigned to God based on a warped view of our father figure. Jesus reveals the Father in a new way; a Father who is present, loving, compassionate and a leader we can trust.

Jesus proclaims:
"If you have seen me, you have seen the Father."

Leaders in the Kingdom exhibit more than just qualities of leadership the world esteems. There is something beyond current leadership strategies that spiritual leaders demonstrate. As Jesus walked the earth with the ordinary people of His day, He demonstrated the heart of the Father. When He healed the blind man, He demonstrated the Father's heart. When He ministered life to the leper, He demonstrated the Father's heart. When He defended the woman caught in adultery, He revealed the Father's heart to us. Real leaders in the Kingdom are fathers.

REAL LEADERS IN THE KINGDOM ARE FATHERS

In the Bible, we see that giving is a quality and characteristic of the Father. He constantly gives; He gives us love, opportunities, forgiveness, second chances, wisdom, and the list goes on and on. Just like all good, natural fathers, I love to give gifts to my children. It brings me so much joy and contentment when I see my daughter and sons receive gifts. Our Father rejoices over us in the same way. This is a quality we get from Him through God's institution of family, which when done in a healthy way is a picture of what the Father desires with us. God is a giver. God so loved the world that He gave us the Son. He is a good Father.

JESUS CAME TO REVEAL THE FATHER

> "No one has ever gazed upon the fullness of God's splendor except the uniquely beloved Son, who is cherished by the Father and held close to his heart. Now he has unfolded to us the full explanation of who God truly is!"
>
> John 1:18 (TPT)

As a leader, Jesus exhibits, demonstrates and represents His Father in everything He does. He also provides us with the model of how He operated in His daily life.

> "So Jesus said, 'I speak to you timeless truth. The Son is not able to do anything from himself or through my own initiative. I only do the works that I see the Father doing, for the Son does the same works as his Father. Because the Father loves his Son so much, he always reveals to me everything that he is about to do. And you will all be amazed when he shows me even greater works than what you've seen so far! For just like the Father has power to raise the dead, the Son will raise the dead and give life to whomever he wants. The Father now judges no one, for he has given all the authority to judge to the Son, so that the honor that belongs to the Father will now be shared with his Son. So if you refuse to honor the Son, you are refusing to honor the Father who sent him. I speak to you an eternal truth: if you embrace my message and believe in the One who sent me, you will never face

condemnation, for in me, you have already passed from the realm of death into the realm of eternal life!'"

John 5:19-24 (TPT)

Jesus states, "The Son can do nothing of Himself, unless it is something He sees the Father doing" (John 5:19). We have examined earlier that Jesus sought solitude in the early morning hours. While Jesus spent time with His Father daily, before He departed His place of prayer to begin ministering to the people, He already knew where He would be going and what He would be doing.

> "…for the Son does the same works as His Father"
>
> John 5:19 (TPT)

Jesus carries and reveals the Father's heart to all He comes in contact with. This is what we are called to do as leaders in the Kingdom.

Leaders in the Kingdom carry and reveal the Father's heart

ONENESS WITH THE FATHER

"'If you had known Me, you would have known My Father also; from now on you know Him, and have seen Him.' Philip said to Him, 'Lord, show us the Father, and it is enough for us.' Jesus said to him, 'Have I been so long with you, and yet you have not come to know Me, Philip? He who has seen Me has seen the Father; how can you say, 'Show us the Father'? Do you not believe that I am in the Father, and the Father is in Me? The words that I say to you I do not speak on My own initiative, but the Father abiding in Me does His works. Believe Me that I am in the Father and the Father is in Me; otherwise believe because of the works themselves. Truly, truly, I say to you, he who believes in Me, the works that I do, he will do also; and greater works than these he will do; because I go to the Father. Whatever you ask in My name, that will I do, so that the Father may be glorified in the Son. If you ask Me anything in My name, I will do it. If you love Me, you will keep My commandments.'"

John 14:7-15

Jesus shows us that He is in union with the Father, and apart from the Father He can do nothing. Just as He lives in union with His Father, His will for us is that we would live in union with Him. In John chapter 15, He gives us a picture of a vine. Jesus is the vine and we are the branches connected to Him. If we stay connected, we bear fruit and yield a harvest.

Jesus is our model of the Father, and as leaders we are to demonstrate the same attributes and characteristics that Jesus modeled for us as He revealed His Father.

COACHING

For men who walk with Jesus and know Him as Lord, our mandate is to carry, display and demonstrate the heart of the Father everywhere we go. That starts in our own family, first and foremost. Just as Jesus displays the Father's heart, we are to love our wives just as Jesus loves His church. We are to lead our families with the tender touch of the Father, balanced with firm correction, raising our children in the way they should go and grow. For many men, we lean on outdated concepts of fathering or call on our past recollections of the way we were parented (which doesn't always meet the standard). We need to seek the scriptures and spend time with our Heavenly Father so we are able to model proper fathering in our families. Demonstrating the Father's heart is not only for our family. We are called to carry the Father's heart in the marketplace, our business, relationships and daily lives.

Book III | Communication

THE **CHISEL**

JESUS IS THE MASTER COMMUNICATOR
———————

JESUS THE STORYTELLER
———————

JESUS HAS A SENSE OF HUMOR
———————

JESUS SPEAKS IN MYSTERIES THAT INVITE DISCOVERY
———————

JESUS IS A FRIEND
———————

JESUS IS A MENTOR
———————

JESUS HAS AN INNER CIRCLE

"Jesus went throughout all of Galilee, teaching in their synagogues, preaching the gospel of the kingdom, and healing all kinds of disease and sickness among the people."

Matthew 4:23 (NET)

JESUS IS THE MASTER COMMUNICATOR

Jesus was revolutionary in the way He communicated. We have many documented encounters of Jesus communicating in various places and to people of varied social status. He is accessible to all. We can learn by observing how He masterfully adapts His approach, using a wide array of linguistic tools and approaches to break social norms and break through into the hearts of people. He captures their attention not only with His content, but also with the manner in which He shares, speaks and listens.

John chapter three records the story of a respected teacher of the law who visited Jesus at night. Nicodemus, a respected Pharisee and ruler among the Jews, makes his approach under a darkened sky to investigate more about this man who performs miracles among the people. As Nicodemus draws near, he opens his visit with a statement acknowledging that Jesus was sent from God. Jesus matches the communication rhythm and responds back with a statement to Nicodemus.

Jesus answered,

> "Truly, truly, I say to you, unless one is born of water and the Spirit he cannot enter into the kingdom of God."
> John 3:3 (NET)

When Jesus makes this statement, it evokes emotion, curiosity and questions. He opens up a dialogue where Nicodemus becomes the pursuer. The more Nicodemus seeks the answers, the more Jesus shares with him. This interaction leads to the earth-shaking statement recorded in John 3:16.

"For this is how much God loved the world—he gave his one and only, unique Son as a gift. So now everyone who believes in him will never perish but experience everlasting life." (TPT)

We can learn a lot about how Jesus shared the good news from an interpersonal perspective. He brings in the supernatural realities of His purpose and destiny to save the world, and at the same time uses logic to reason and appeal to Nicodemus' inability to grasp what is being discussed. Jesus pulls Nicodemus into a deep spiritual dialogue. Jesus pulls people closer and speaks to the seeker. Earnest seekers have the most engaging dialogue with Jesus. He never pushes or forces His way into our lives. Instead, He provokes thought and His words are delivered in a way that demands a response.

Jesus always pulls people towards truth, He doesn't push

Jesus is the master communicator. His words strike us to the core and radically impact us. Jesus is God's Word in living form. John chapter one states that the 'Word' became flesh and dwelt among us. Jesus is the living embodiment of the Father's message to us. We could say that Jesus is the Father's ultimate love letter to all of humanity. It is impossible to hear the Word of God and remain unchanged. The Bible records that God's Word will not return void; it will do what it was sent out to do. In the book of Hebrews, God's Word is described as a sword.

> "For the word of God is living and active and sharper than any two-edged sword, and piercing as far as the division of soul and spirit, of both joints and marrow, and able to judge the thoughts and intentions of the heart."
>
> Hebrews 4:12

The words of Jesus changed those who heard them, and they can change us today. He challenges, draws and provokes us. In the Bible, Jeremiah creates the image of God as the potter and us as the clay. That is an accurate picture, since His desire is to mold and shape us.

Jesus was a builder for the majority of His life. One of the tools He would have carried is the chisel. A chisel is used to chip away at an object until its inner beauty is revealed. A chisel in the hands of an unskilled laborer can do massive damage, breaking and scarring the raw material. The chisel in the hand of a master craftsman shapes a natural substance into something useful and with a purpose decided by the one who wields this tool. When Jesus speaks to us, His words and presence are like a chisel, chipping away at the substance that is not needed to reveal His intent for our lives. Let's look at His communication style: not only at His spoken words, but also the other ways He communicates and relates to those around Him.

SEE JESUS AS THE MASTER COMMUNICATOR.

"All these things Jesus spoke to the crowds in parables, and He did not speak to them without a parable."

Matthew 13:34

JESUS THE STORYTELLER

Neuroscience is now proving that storytelling is a very effective manner of communication that activates our brains and increases the way we process, engage and retain information. Telling a story is beneficial for building deep relationships. In the world of marketing, 'story' is being used to forge deeper connections, and in sales, story is used to build trust and exert influence. It is through stories that we understand each other in deeper ways. When stories are told correctly, they frame context, inspire curiosity, help us visualize the experience that is being shared, evoke our emotions, and build trust.

JESUS IS THE MASTER STORYTELLER

Jesus is extremely relational and relatable. He did not cloak Himself in degrees, and He didn't study to become a rabbi. Instead, He spent His teenage years and His 20's earning a living as a builder. Throughout His life, He would accumulate many human experiences and observe behavior that shaped the way He chose to relate to His audience when teaching. He made Kingdom truths accessible through ordinary, day-to-day examples that His hearers would be thoroughly familiar with. He tells stories in a way that invites discovery and requires something of the hearers. He looked for those willing to search beyond the surface levels to receive the full meaning of what He taught. Jesus' preferred teaching method was through parables and stories that illustrate deeper spiritual truths. Parables are earthly stories that carry a spiritual meaning.

- Parables initiate and invite listeners into discovery.
- Parables illuminate and inspire the search for truth.
- Parables reveal intelligence and offer instruction.

Let's talk more about these concepts and see how Jesus masterfully uses them.

After teaching the listeners the Parable of the Seed and Sower, Matthew records the following interaction between Jesus and His disciples.

> "Then his disciples approached Jesus and asked, "Why do you always speak to people in these hard-to-understand parables?" "He explained, 'You've been given the intimate experience of insight into the hidden truths and mysteries of the realm of heaven's kingdom, but they have not. For everyone who listens with an open heart will receive progressively more revelation until he has more than enough. But those who don't listen with an open, teachable heart, even the understanding that they think they have will be taken from them. That's why I teach the people using parables, because they think they're looking for truth, yet because their hearts are unteachable, they never discover it. Although they will listen to me, they never fully perceive the message I speak.'"
>
> Matthew 13:10-13 (TPT)

This is a powerful and revealing statement from the mouth of Jesus. His disciples are privileged to receive secret, closed-door insights through their mentorship from Jesus. The Message Bible states the same passage this way:

> "The disciples came up and asked, 'Why do you tell stories?' He replied, 'You've been given insight into God's kingdom. You know how it works. Not everybody has this gift, this insight; it hasn't been given to them. Whenever someone has a ready heart for this, the insights and understandings flow freely. But if there is no readiness, any trace of receptivity soon disappears. That's why I tell stories: to create readiness, to nudge the people toward receptive insight. In their present state they can stare till doomsday and not see it, listen till they're blue in the face and not get it.'"
>
> Matthew 13:10-13 (MSG)

With Jesus' words we see that He is interested in seekers. He tells His listeners to, "Seek first the Kingdom." Jesus is attracted to and attracts the earnest and the open. His message is available to all, but it draws the spiritually curious. The parables He teaches will require humility. The teachings of Jesus are not meant to be sampled like food at a buffet meal. His message is polarizing and requires a response. Jesus made it difficult to be a passive listener. After teaching the crowds the parable of the lamp, He proceeds to provide a warning to those within the sound of His voice.

> "So pay careful attention to your hearts as you hear my teaching, for to those who have open hearts, even more revelation will be given to them until it overflows. And for those who do not listen with open hearts, what little light they imagine to have will be taken away."
> Luke 8:18 (TPT)

We are responsible for what we hear in the Kingdom. Revelation knowledge is never imparted for entertainment purposes. The Word is sent forth with a specific mission. If we do not steward what we hear and obey what is taught, we will stop receiving more.

COACHING

My favorite line in Spiderman is when Uncle Ben tells Peter Parker that "with great power comes great responsibility." This famous movie line is similar to the Kingdom principle Jesus imparts; the principle that we are responsible for what we know. After Jesus heals a blind man, Jesus provokes the Pharisees with the following statement:

> "And Jesus said, 'For judgment I came into this world, so that those who do not see may see, and that those who see may become blind.' Those of the Pharisees who were with Him heard these things and said to Him, 'We are not blind too, are we?'"

Look how Jesus responds;

> "Jesus said to them, 'If you were blind, you would have no sin; but since you say, 'We see,' your sin remains.'"
>
> John 9:39-41

Many men acknowledge God with their mouth, on the bios of their social media profiles and in the post-game interview, but their seat in church is empty every Sunday, living a self-centered life, lacking faith and the evidence it produces. I am not casting stones at anyone who makes an outward profession of being a follower of Jesus. In the Kingdom we are responsible for what we do, not what we portray. There will come a day where we will be held accountable for our words and actions. It's easy to accept Jesus as your Savior; it's a harder decision to make Him Lord in your life.

"…to grant those who mourn in Zion, giving them a garland instead of ashes, the oil of gladness instead of mourning…"

Isaiah 61:3

JESUS HAS A SENSE OF HUMOR

Within the pages of Scripture, we read there is a time to laugh. God is the author of our emotions, and He created you and I with the ability for enjoyment and laughter. Joy is one of the fruits of the Spirit (Galatians 5). There is no doubt that Jesus laughed and enjoyed Himself as a man, and I'm sure He also enjoyed seeing others laugh and smile.

JESUS USES PUNS, PLAYS ON WORDS AND WORD PICTURES

When you approach the New Testament with a fresh lens, you can see that Jesus had an awesome personality. He is far from the emotionless, stoic character religion would lead you to believe He is. One of the ways we can gain insight into His personality and playfulness is found in the way He uses language and analogy. This is often lost for us English readers because of our various Bible translations. The original language is rich and deep, and as with any foreign language there are double meanings, cultural references and plays on words that are often not accurately transferable through a translation. Jesus loves to use puns, plays on words and word pictures to illustrate His teachings. Through His use of language, we get a deeper picture of His personality, playfulness and sense of humor.

After Jesus chooses Phillip as one of His disciples, Phillip found Nathaniel and tells him the good news that Jesus is the long-awaited Messiah Moses and the Prophets wrote about. Nathaniel's gut reaction is;

> "Can any good thing come out of Nazareth?"
>
> John 1:46

After Nathaniel makes this sarcastic statement and agrees to go and meet Jesus, Jesus makes the following declaration upon seeing Nathaniel:

> "Behold, an Israelite indeed, in whom there is no deceit!"
>
> John 1:47

Jesus makes this statement as a play on words regarding the Old Testament Jacob who was known as a man of guile and deceit before God renamed Him Israel (Genesis 27:35, 31:26). His use of humor instantly engages Nathaniel as Jesus is hand-picking His 12 disciples.

GET A NEW NAME

Guys often see qualities in each other and assign nicknames to label each other based on these qualities we exhibit. Oftentimes it has a touch of humor in it. Jesus chose to walk with 12 men who were immersed in the marketplace and commonplace culture of the day. Many were from the fishing industry, which would be considered far from a religious environment. He uses a pun to explain how they would now be "fishers of men."

Jesus refers to the brothers, James and John, as the 'Sons of Thunder,' which could also be translated as the 'sons of commotion.' These two brothers are extreme in their approach by preventing people to cast out demons (Mark 9:38) and requesting to call down fire on a village who didn't receive His message (Luke 9:54). You can almost see Jesus wince and maybe chuckle to Himself as He corrects these two, assigning them their new nickname.

Jesus renames Simon Peter to Cephas, which is often understood to be translated as a stone or rock. Peter was the hard-headed, stubborn guy who always jumped in head first into every situation. Knowing full well who Peter was and the behavior he exhibits, it is amusing in and of itself that His nickname is 'The Rock.'

BLIND GUIDES

Then there are the Pharisees, who constantly harass Jesus everywhere He goes. Whenever He taught in public…there they are, lurking in the background, analyzing every claim, attempting to set traps that provide the 'aha' moment they have been waiting for. Jesus labels these religious leaders as 'blind guides,' which most likely would have entertained the crowds.

EXTREME ANALOGIES

Jesus uses exaggerated analogies to paint hilarious pictures that would have illustrated His point and made the crowds laugh.

> "What happens when a blind man pretends to guide another blind man? They both stumble into a ditch! And how could the apprentice know more than his master, for only after he is fully qualified will he be at that level. Why do you focus on the flaw in someone else's life and fail to notice the glaring flaws of your own life? How could you say to your friend, 'Here, let me show you where you're wrong,' when you are guilty of even more than he is? You are overly critical, splitting hairs and being a hypocrite! You must acknowledge your own blind spots and deal with them before you will be able to deal with the blind spot of your friend."
>
> Luke 6:39-42 (TPT)

COACHING

We don't have to always be "on." Dedicate time to have fun, laugh and be entertained with friends you can loosen up with. We should expect to have fun. Laughing and having fun is part of the resting process and is a benefit of great fellowship together.

It is also important to include boundaries that we do not cross in the name of a good laugh. It can be a slippery slope once we enter into a gray area with our humor. The men in the early church were not that different from you and I. The issues they faced and what they had to be on guard against still remain for us today. Consider Paul's warning to the churches in Ephesus.

> "…and there must be no filthiness and silly talk, or coarse jesting, which are not fitting, but rather giving of thanks."
>
> Ephesians 5:4

Humor allows us to:

- Not take ourselves so seriously
- Show vulnerability
- Be relatable

"It is the glory of God to conceal a matter, but the glory of kings is to search out a matter."

———

Proverbs 25:2

HE SPEAKS IN MYSTERIES THAT INVITE DISCOVERY

Jesus compares the Kingdom of Heaven to treasure that was hidden in a field, where the person who discovers the treasure goes and sells all that he has to purchase the field and the treasure within. In the same discourse, He compares the Kingdom of Heaven to a merchant seeking fine pearls, who when he finds one, sells all that he has to purchase this pearl of great price.

One of the major themes Jesus teaches to His listeners is the concept of seeking. In His teaching on prayer, He encourages His listeners to ask, seek and knock. The picture is one of a continual seeking until you find that what you are in search of. There is even an anagram wrapped in the English translation of Ask-Seek-Knock (A-S-K). Jesus also instructed people to seek first the Kingdom of God. It's as though there is a latent, divine curiosity we all possess that Jesus seeks to awaken in the lives of those who hear His words.

Throughout Scripture, in both the Old and New Testament, there is a conditional principle that surfaces and is continually in front of us. We see through the story of Israel in the Old Testament, the conditions that God gave Israel. Over and over God relays His messages through His spokespeople, the prophets, who were constantly calling the nation back to God, foretelling what would happen based on how they received the message. For example, If the nation would turn back to God, the promise of great blessing and abundance would be experienced. Likewise, if the nation rejected God's commands, there would be a consequence, such as famine, pestilence or war.

It was a conditional 'if → then' relationship.

Have you ever wondered why Jesus ended so many parables with this phrase: "He who has ears to hear, let him hear"? We all have physical ears, so what is Jesus referring to? This is another example of Jesus calling people to the truth in public. He openly invites, draws and provokes the curiosity of the crowds, but not all respond. He came to His own people first, but they all did not receive Him. "He who has ears to hear, let him hear" is the conditional request of Jesus to all who hear His voice, like the modern-day equivalent of saying, "Listen up," or "Pay attention." Jesus is accessible, yet this disclosure has an exclusionary component. Even though everyone gets access to the teachings, Jesus is calling the attentive, the curious and the earnest seekers to full attention. Let's look at how Bible translators have interpreted this curious saying of Jesus.

Mark 4:9

"He who has ears to be hearing, let him be hearing."
Wuest

"Are you listening to this? Really listening?"
The Message

"Whoever has ears to hear had better listen!"
NET Bible

"If you understand this, then you need to respond."
The Passion Translation

These are conditional statements and are invitational in nature. You are invited into the offer if you meet the conditions. In the case of Jesus sharing these new spiritual truths the offer to step into the new reality of this Kingdom realm is for those who respond.

In Mark chapter four's Parable of the Sower, Jesus teaches the crowds. Jesus instructs them to listen and invites them to consider what He is teaching. He tells about four scenarios of a farmer sowing seed. No further explanation is given. The deep truths of what He teaches will be kept out of reach of the casual follower. With every word wrapped in riddle, He is inviting those who have ears to hear to go deeper.

In Mark 4:11, the disciples ask Jesus more about the parables, and this is how Jesus responds:

> "And He was saying to them, 'To you has been given the mystery of the kingdom of God, but those who are outside get everything in parables, so that while seeing, they may see and not perceive, and while hearing, they may hear and not understand, otherwise they might return and be forgiven.'"
>
> Mark 4:11

Jesus quotes a portion of Isaiah 6 that speaks of people who have made the choice to ignore the Word of the Lord. Craig Keener, in the IVP Bible Background Commentary: New Testament, states that:

> "Jewish teachers normally used parables to illustrate and explain points, not to conceal them. But if one tells stories without stating the point they were meant to illustrate, as Jesus does here, only those who listen most astutely (4:9) and start with insiders' knowledge could possibly figure out one's point. The members of the Qumran community believed that God gave secrets to the prophets that they encoded in the Bible, and that God revealed the interpretation of those biblical texts to their own teacher, who shared it only with them. Greek teachers like Plato and sometimes Jewish teachers would leave certain points obscure to keep them from outsiders; only those who were serious enough to persevere would understand."

Brian Simmons has a note in The Passion Translation referring to 'the outsiders' or those who hear without understanding (TPT note, Mark 4:11-12):

"The Aramaic is 'backward ones.' Jesus spoke allegorically so that those who didn't care to understand couldn't understand. Yet He knew that the hungry ones would seek out the hidden meaning of the parables and understand the secrets of God's kingdom realm. It is still that way today."

Jesus instructs His disciples to:

"Be diligent to understand the meaning behind everything you hear, for as you do, more understanding will be given to you. And according to the depth of your longing to understand, much more will be added to you. For those who listen with open hearts will receive more revelation. But those who don't listen with open hearts will lose what little they think they have!"

Mark 4:24-25 (TPT)

A RESPONSE IS REQUIRED

In the Kingdom, this is the proper order: seek first the Kingdom, and then more will be given. There is an instruction for us to take care and be diligent in seeking the meaning of what we hear. The principle applies to us today. As we have already discussed, we are accountable for what we hear and what has been given to us. There is a responsibility that comes with new revelation and knowledge. If we do not apply what we have heard and learn to walk in it, the implication is that we will not receive more.

COACHING

We have been privileged to discover the deeper meanings of Jesus' teachings through the Word of God. Like the disciples, we get a front-row seat through their accounts of Jesus as He breaks down explanations and hidden meanings behind His parables. Once we gain insight to the truth, we are now responsible for what we know. What I have observed and learned through scripture and walking with the Lord is that promises and words from God are conditional.

To access the fullness of all that is available to us in this life, in both the spiritual and natural realm, there are conditions, there are 'if's.' As in if you do 'X,' then 'Y' will happen. I am not reducing God's Word to a formula meant to be hacked. However, you cannot deny that our behaviors dictate outcomes. If you touch a hot stove, you will get burned! If I deny my flesh and pick up my cross daily, I can expect to align with God's will for my life. The Bible is full of if/then statements, and to deny that God has conditional promises is foolishness. The question now becomes what are the 'if's' that God is specifically speaking to you?

"...but there is a friend who sticks closer than a brother."

Proverbs 18:24

JESUS IS A FRIEND

Jesus is the ultimate friend. In His earthly ministry, He initiated and developed intimate friendships with his followers. He served as their leader, coach, mentor and above all, Lord. Among all of these titles, He also stands out as their friend.

During the last Passover before being betrayed by Judas, Jesus states His betrayer is someone who has dipped the bread in the cup with Him. This is a reference to someone who has shared meals with Him as an intimate friend. Jesus would have shared hundreds of meals over three years with His disciples. They would have taken many walks together from one city to the next. There would be time spent in prayer with each other, early morning reflections, intimate discussions into the dark hours of the night, and they would even sing together (Mark 14:26).

On one such occasion during the last Passover, in a private venue secluded from the outside world, Jesus shares the secrets of what will unfold over the coming days. This scene is recorded in John chapters 13 and 14. It is an intimate gathering of friends, where Jesus will wash the disciples' feet, recline at a table for a meal and share secrets the world had never known and only the disciples were privileged to hear. Within these chapters, we get a view of how Jesus interacts with His closest friends. We have an image presented of John leaning with his head resting on the chest of Jesus. What a picture of a loving Lord. He loves us; He is comforting and we can lean on Him. He is not distant or afraid to be close with others. He is the friend who sticks closer than a brother.

Shortly after this scene, Jesus continues sharing the secrets of His Kingdom. Jesus tells His disciples that He does not call them servants, but they are now his intimate friends.

> "So this is my command: Love each other deeply, as much as I have loved you. For the greatest love of all is a love that sacrifices all. And this great love is demonstrated when a person sacrifices his life for his friends. You show that you are my intimate friends when you obey all that I command you. I have never called you 'servants,' because a master doesn't confide in his servants, and servants don't always understand what the master is doing. But I call you my most intimate friends, for I reveal to you everything that I've heard from my Father."
> John 15:12-15 (TPT)

The use of the word 'friends' here can also be compared to close family or a relative. Jesus is friendship. He never lets us down, and this term encapsulates the close bond that He desires to have with us. Men need friends. We are hard wired to enjoy the company of other guys who have shared interests. As we laugh and open up about aspirations, dreams, challenges and even our setbacks, we develop the bonds of friendship. Our network and support system strengthen us and we no longer feel the loneliness and isolation the enemy tries to lure us into.

One of the most powerful aspects of the model Jesus gave us relationally is community. He gathered his tribe, walked out life with them and founded the ecclesia (His church) in a model of community rather than isolation. You were never meant to walk out the Christian life alone. The power is in community, and within community you will discover and develop deep, powerful friendships. One of my mentors calls this concept of community 'the natural habitat of the Christian.' A species cannot survive for long (and certainly cannot remain strong and thrive) once removed from their habitat and natural surroundings.

COACHING

BEWARE OF ISOLATION

It is the enemy's desire to separate and isolate. As men we can sometimes choose isolation over community and relationship. Don't make this mistake! Deep spiritual growth and maturity is found in community. The model Jesus provides and the life of the first century church clearly shows the importance of sharing life together. Times have changed, and life in the 21st Century is certainly different, posing challenges and barriers to forging deep, meaningful connections.

We are more connected than ever, surrounded by crowds of people and wired through our social networks, yet this has not solved the feelings of loneliness. The solution is community. The church is not a building; it is His body. Decide to step out of your comfort zone and attend gatherings with other like-minded believers. Get involved, plug in, go to a home group, a Bible study, and volunteer. You will not find perfect Christians, completely incapable of offending you, but you will discover God's intent for how the Christian life is to be lived and shared: with others.

"A pupil is not above his teacher; but everyone, after he has been fully trained, will be like his teacher."

Luke 6:40

JESUS IS A MENTOR

The word 'rabbi' can be translated as 'teacher.' The eastern view of following a teacher is much more expansive than our view of a teacher in the west. The eastern mindset values experience over informational head knowledge typical in classroom settings. To follow a Rabbi in the Jewish culture was to watch, observe, participate and be fully immersed into an apprenticeship-like relationship. Think of it more like mentorship than teaching in the traditional, western sense.

A mentor is an experienced, trusted advisor – someone who offers participation into an experience with opportunity for dialogue to increase our understanding. This is what Jesus models and does today. Whether you are in the Middle-Eastern culture in the times of Jesus or you're in the present-day business or church culture, the rules remain the same for mentorship. The mentor/mentee relationship is always driven by the mentee. The student must be the pursuer, or the relationship fails. The relationship can be initiated by the mentor, but must be driven by the mentee. An example of this is when Jesus tells Nathaniel "come follow me."

The premise of all mentorships is that the mentor possesses something the mentee desires, so the mentee humbles themselves, is teachable and desires coaching from the mentor. The dynamic in this relationship is the more the mentee pulls on the mentor, the more they will receive. There is a humility exhibited: first to approach and acknowledge a need for mentorship, and then the pursuing to initiate teaching and coaching. The hungrier the student is, the more they can receive.

Mentorships are time bound and should have established boundaries, rules of engagement and agreed operating principles. Jesus models mentoring. The entire three years of Jesus' life with the disciples is considered mentoring. They observed Jesus as Lord, leader, coach and teacher. They got an up-close and personal view to His way of life.

In this dynamic, at a specific point in time, the mentee is released and now becomes a mentor for others.

COACHING

Identify an area in your life that the Lord is highlighting to you. This could be an area of opportunity where you need to develop yourself, or it could be an area you are proficient in already, but could benefit from someone's wisdom who has more experience.

Once you identify this area, can you think of a man who you could benefit from learning from? Start with a coffee or lunch meeting to explore if this person could be a mentor in this area.

Remember, all mentorships should be time bound, so when you choose to move forward as the mentor or the mentee in this relationship, set clear expectations and boundaries with a start/stop date to alleviate an awkward situation once the mentorship is over. These relationships are seldom meant to go on forever.

You can have multiple mentors for various skill sets you need. Try to have no more than two mentorships going on at once, but you certainly do not have to limit yourself to only one area and one mentor.

I have served others as mentor and also have sought the wisdom of others by pursuing a mentor. It is important to understand that you do not need a relationship with the person you are seeking mentorship from. I consider myself to be mentored by multiple people that have served me as 'distance mentors.' I have never met these authors, speakers or leaders, but I have diligently sought out and invested in their material and applied what they have taught me.

Regardless of whether you choose a direct or indirect mentor, find the person who has the wisdom you need and follow their advice.

"Six days later Jesus took with Him Peter and James and John his brother, and led them up on a high mountain by themselves."

Matthew 17:1

JESUS HAS AN INNER CIRCLE

Among your friendships, you should always have a core group of your two to three closest relationships. This is your inner circle. For Jesus, Peter, James and John formed His inner circle; relationships that witnessed His most private moments. These three men shared some of the most exceptional experiences recorded in Scripture and no doubt other private conversations, teachings and mentorship moments not recorded within the pages of the Bible.

Peter and the two brothers, James and John, are called to go behind the curtain when Jesus leaves the other nine disciples to go minister to Jarius' daughter (Mark 5:37). The three will witness the physically dead rise and get the privilege of being mentored through observation and participation in the atmosphere of resurrection. They are called apart to ascend the high mountain with Jesus as they march to the place where He is transfigured and His glory is revealed (Matthew 17:1-8). They experience an awe-filled spiritual encounter with Moses and Elijah as their ears open to hear the Father's voice from heaven. They get to see Jesus physically illuminated as He openly declares His Lordship from a mountain top in Israel.

In His darkest hour, Jesus calls upon Peter, James and John to go further into the Garden of Gethsemane, while He reveals deep emotion and bears His heart and innermost feelings before being crucified. They will be within proximity of the Savior of all humanity as He makes preparation for the epic events that will transpire within the next 24 hours (Matthew 26:37). These three men get to participate in a circle of trust and friendship that brings comfort to Jesus.

The purpose of the inner circle also serves these men. Imagine this high-level mastermind and mentorship, where Jesus pours into these leaders and views them from their future. These men have an appointed destiny within the Kingdom of God and are governmental leaders who will serve the church in the office of Apostle. John will reveal the love of Jesus like no other in his Gospel account of their time together. He will also write one of the most important letters concerning the end times and ultimate destiny of the church in the book of Revelation. Peter will transform from simple, strong-headed fisherman to the chief Apostle to the Jews. James will go to preach and help establish the foundations of the early church in Jerusalem and Judea. He will later be beheaded by Herod Agrippa (Acts 12:2).

Jesus provides a powerful model of the importance of close friendships and allowing those you lead into your process. By investing His time with Peter, James and John. Jesus demonstrates that leaders go the extra mile with their students, sharing life and providing deeper instruction to those they develop. These three men get the benefit of private teaching, behind the scenes mentoring and live within the model of how to raise up other leaders. As a result of this relationship, these three men will model what they have been invited to participate in with Jesus.

PETER

Peter is a leader and raises up other leaders and believers. He boldly proclaims the Gospel message on the day of Pentecost and leads many to Christ. He becomes the chief apostle to the Jews. He ministers, oversees and writes two letters to the newly-formed churches with 1st and 2nd Peter. He also mentors others like he was mentored by Jesus. Peter mentors Mark like a father. Mark's Gospel is a record of Peter's teaching. Mark acted as Peter's scribe and becomes like a son to Peter.

> "She who is in Babylon, chosen together with you, sends you greetings, and so does my son, Mark."
>
> 1 Peter 5:13

JOHN

John also ministers to believers and raises up and oversees the early church. In addition to writing the Gospel of John and the book of Revelation, He writes three additional letters with 1st, 2nd and 3rd John to encourage and instruct others. Although it is not found within the Bible, church tradition records that John trained Polycarp who later became Bishop of Smyrna. Polycarp carried John's teachings to future generations and raised up other leaders in a similar pattern to how John fathered him.

We can measure the impact and leadership legacy that these men left as a result of their close relationship with Jesus.

COACHING

Your inner circle can change. Many times throughout a man's life, due to new relationships, life experiences and relocations, the people brought into your life shifts. There will be seasons where you may be surrounded with one or two people who become your good friends or advisors for some of your life situations. Be aware that your inner circle can move and change as you grow and change. Your close relationships do not have to be within close physical proximity to you. I have very close friends, as well as those I consider mentors and counselors who I speak and connect with through texting, email, video and social media. Friendships take work. There is an investment of time, listening and attention on both sides, especially inside your 'inner circle.'

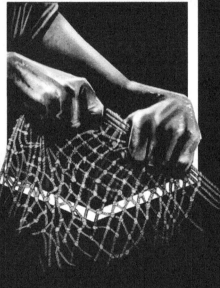

Book IV
Empathy

THE FISHING NET

THE FISHER OF MEN
———
JESUS SHOWS EMOTION
———
JESUS MODELS ALL OF THE FRUIT OF THE SPIRIT
———
JESUS LIBERATES WOMEN
———
JESUS IS GENTLE
———
JESUS MODEL'S HUMILITY
———
JESUS IS A MAN OF COMPASSION
———
JESUS DEFENDS THE WEAK
———
JESUS FORGIVES AND RESTORES

"Then Jesus said to them, 'Follow Me, and I will make you become fishers of men.'"

———

Mark 1:17

THE FISHER OF MEN

Jesus uses the imagery of reaping a harvest. When He saw the spiritually hungry crowds coming towards Him He told His disciples "Now is the Harvest time!" He explained that their hearts are like fields that are ripened and ready to be harvested, and that those who reap in the harvest will have a reward (John 4:35). When Jesus was calling His disciples, He uses the language of the fishing industry to relate the opportunity of offering salvation through the message of His Kingdom. Everything Jesus does produces results. Everywhere the Kingdom goes it makes an impact, Jesus relates this through parabolic teaching when He speaks of the harvest and producing good fruit. Jesus is relational, this is how He reaches people, connects with those around Him and draws them to the Father. Jesus stated:

> "And I, when I am lifted up from the earth, will draw all people to myself."
>
> John 12:32 (NET)

Jesus understands people and their situations. He is in tune with where they have been and what they need. He initiates and responds in a way that makes people feel valued and valuable. I believe Jesus loves us each so much as individuals that if you were literally the only one on earth, Jesus would still have died on the cross just for you. He is a caring Savior.

Jesus is emotionally intelligent. Emotional intelligence or E.Q. can be defined as the ability to identify and manage one's own emotions, as well as the emotions of others. E.Q. is one of the number one determinants of success for anyone who works with people, whether you are in ministry, sales, the medical field and most certainly formal leadership positions.

Jesus shows emotion, but as men we were not all raised, encouraged or given permission to display our emotions; specifically the emotions that show our sensitivity. You may have been taunted at the playground or even by an authority figure with sayings like, "Don't be a cry baby," "Real men don't cry," "Don't act like a girl," and, "Suck it up." Our faux masculine culture has taught generations of boys that men can't be in touch with their feelings, especially when those feelings move us towards revealing anything perceived as weakness. It is common to see today's male wearing an alpha male mask in attempt to demonstrate masculine energy, overcompensating for wounds and being careful to never show weakness or reveal insecurities.

As we will see, Jesus expressed a range of human emotions. You were created with emotions, and we can learn from watching Jesus how He expressed those emotions in various circumstances to impact those around Him and express Himself.

There also exists a false notion of an emotionless Jesus, a stoic figure who ministers from a distance, a man who is neither sad nor happy. Stoicism is based on the ancient Greek philosophers who governed by logic and natural reasoning in a non-emotional manner. This emotionless, stained-glass version of Jesus has been depicted in art across the centuries. This version of Jesus is distant, not connected and unrelatable to most. This 'religious' replica of the genuine Jesus has shaped and infiltrated some of the largest institutional religious systems and culture telling us that we must check our emotions at the door. As we take a closer look, let's see how this is unbiblical and certainly not the model Jesus provides.

"So, chosen by God for this new life of love, dress in the wardrobe God picked out for you: compassion, kindness, humility, quiet strength, discipline."

Colossians 3:12 (MSG)

JESUS SHOWS EMOTION

Jesus is a real man who never attempts to hide His emotion or mask His feelings. We observe Jesus walk out the range of human emotion. Here are just a few examples of the many times we can read about Jesus displaying His emotions.

- Jesus marveled at the Centurion's faith.
- Jesus was angry when He flipped the tables.
- Jesus displays humor through the puns and word pictures He uses.
- Jesus was deeply moved in spirit and with compassion on the way to see Lazarus.
- Jesus weeps over Jerusalem and is not afraid show emotion and even cry in front of others.
- Jesus was moved with indignation and was grieved at the hardness of heart of the Pharisees

We live in a day where it is now the norm to give people a fraction of attention while we scroll through our phones and multi-task. Jesus was 100% dialed in to the person He was engaging. He was no respecter of persons and treated each person with dignity and respect. Imagine what it must have been like when He was playing with the children, seeing Him stoop down to eye level, giving them all of His attention, unconcerned with what others thought. He told them stories and told others that they must become like these little ones. He was also a fierce defender of the children, once saying it would be better to have a millstone tied around your neck and be thrown into the sea than to harm one of these little ones. He stands up for the defenseless. He is our model of a real man.

EMPATHY

Jesus moved with empathy. Wikipedia defines empathy as, "The capacity to understand or feel what another person is experiencing from within their frame of reference, that is, the capacity to place oneself in another's position." In certain professions, such as doctors, counselors and teachers, empathy is a valuable characteristic to have in order to make a meaningful connection with the person you are working with.

This is exactly what we see Jesus do. Jesus has the ability to see and enter someone's experience without being restricted by the emotions He feels. Jesus is a man of compassion. As the Son of Man, He is able to relate to us in all of our human shortcomings. He is patient and He is kind.

SYMPATHY

One important distinction worthy of our discussion is empathy vs. sympathy. We defined empathy as understanding the feelings of another. Sympathy is defined as sharing the feelings of another.

> With empathy, there is an understanding of the emotion.
> With sympathy, there is a participation in the emotion.

Jesus moved with empathy so He could understand others, relate to them and minister to them in their present condition. Jesus did not move in sympathy. He did not share the feelings to the point of participating with the emotion they were feeling. Why not? If He had, it would have impacted His ability to be effective in His ministry.

He could understand the grief of the mourning parents who just got the news that their daughter had died. At the same time, He could still operate in faith and strength despite understanding their emotion. If He had entered into the emotion of grief, it would have impacted His ability to minister. This is important for us to understand as well. Because we are called to be sensitive and exhibit the fruit of the Spirit, we need to understand that operating in sympathy over empathy has the potential to derail our mission and undermine our leadership.

COACHING

As husbands and fathers (whether actual or aspiring to be), it is critical to healthy relationships that we as men can discuss and get comfortable relating our emotions. Most of our relationships are based on how we make others feel. It's not only about the words we speak, but the emotions we transmit through our communication, both verbal and nonverbal. Jesus was comfortable exhibiting His emotions and was in control of His emotional state. Look for opportunities this week to discuss with someone how you are feeling and practice active listening with empathy to those around you.

"But the fruit of the Spirit is love, joy, peace, patience, kindness, goodness, faithfulness, gentleness, self-control; against such things there is no law."

Galatians 5:22-23

JESUS OPERATES AND MODELS ALL THE FRUIT OF THE SPIRIT

Jesus tells His closest followers that the will of His Father is for them to bear much fruit; lasting fruit. Jesus uses the imagery of Him being the vine and His followers are the branches. The instruction is that if they remain in Him, they will produce lasting fruit.

> "I am the vine, you are the branches; he who abides in Me and I in him, he bears much fruit, for apart from Me you can do nothing."
> John 15:5

In the letter to the Galatians, Paul instructs the church to walk by the Spirit so they will not fulfill the desire of the flesh. Paul provides vivid examples of the bad 'fruit' of living a life governed by our fleshly desires.

> "The cravings of the self-life are obvious:
> - sexual immorality
> - lustful thoughts
> - pornography
> - chasing after things instead of God
> - manipulating others
> - hatred of those who get in your way
> - senseless arguments
> - resentment when others are favored
> - temper tantrums
> - angry quarrels
> - only thinking of yourself
> - being in love with your own opinions
> - being envious of the blessings of others
> - murder
> - uncontrolled addictions
> - wild parties
> - and all other similar behavior

"Haven't I already warned you that those who use their 'freedom' for these things will not inherit the kingdom realm of God!"

Galatians 5:19-23 (TPT)

After making this list, Paul progresses to contrast the evidence of walking in the flesh with the fruit of the Spirit. Jesus personified the fruit of the Spirit and modeled what this looked like throughout His earthly ministry. Below is the list of the fruit of the Spirit and examples of how Jesus exhibited each one. My examples are not exhaustive by any means. They are merely a starting point for you to explore and discover the examples Jesus provides.

LOVE

Jesus is love personified, and it was (and is) love that drove His mission. Love led Him to the cross. Love is not merely a characteristic or attribute Jesus exhibited. Jesus is love.

> "Just as the Father has loved Me, I have also loved you; abide in My love. If you keep My commandments, you will abide in My love; just as I have kept My Father's commandments and abide in His love. These things I have spoken to you so that My joy may be in you, and that your joy may be made full. This is My commandment, that you love one another, just as I have loved you. Greater love has no one than this, that one lay down his life for his friends"
>
> *John 15:9-13*

JOY

What kept Jesus focused on the cross throughout His earthly ministry? He never abandoned His mission despite numerous opportunities to do so. The writer of Hebrews shares with us that it was for the joy that was set before Him that He was able to endure the cross and the humiliation of His sufferings.

> "…fixing our eyes on Jesus, the author and perfecter of faith, who for the joy set before Him endured the cross, despising the shame, and

has sat down at the right hand of the throne of God"

Hebrews 12:2

PEACE

One of the titles given to Jesus hundreds of years before He walked the earth as a man is the 'Prince of Peace' (Isaiah 9:6.) He fulfilled this title as He imparted peace to people and situations during His physical life on earth. Even as He healed the blind He brought peace, transferring them from darkness into the light both spiritually and physically. Hear His voice echo, "Peace be still" to the raging storm that attempts to sideline Him from His next ministry destination. Listen to the impartation to His disciples after His resurrection when He declares, "Peace to you" (Luke 24:36, John 20:19). Jesus gives us peace unlike anything this world could ever offer. Jesus directly stated to His disciples,

"Peace I leave with you; My peace I give to you; not as the world gives do I give to you"

John 14:27

PATIENCE

Jesus is incredibly patient. Picture Him walking along the lakeside after ministering and crowds follow Him, pressing Him to the point that He has to get in a boat to speak to them from the water (Mark 3:7). See Him go home to eat a meal with His friends and the crowd follows Him, which includes the religious scholars hurling accusations, while He is physically tired and seeking rest. The word 'patience' used here is associated with endurance. Jesus employs patient endurance with all of those around Him. Even in the midst of a brutal and merciless crucifixion at the hands of His torturers, hear Him cry out as the ultimate evidence of His enduring patience:

"Father, forgive them; for they do not know what they are doing"

Luke 23:34

KINDNESS

We have many examples of Jesus displaying kindness. Every miracle He performed, every word He spoke and every place He visited was an act of kindness. There is one specific example that strikes me as exceptionally kind. During His arrest in the Garden of Gethsemane, a group of temple guards, guided by Judas, arrest Jesus in the dark of night. During this interaction, an over-zealous disciple draws a sword and cuts off the right ear of Malchus, a servant of the high priest. In the midst of this scene Jesus reprimands His disciples and the religious leaders for the physical confrontation and instantly heals the man's ear, and then confronts the chief priests and temple guards.

Consider the context of this act of kindness. This group of men schemed to take Jesus by surprise, under darkness, with brute force, out of the light of day and view of the public eye. They boil over in their hatred for Jesus and His message, yet despite this, Jesus brings healing to every causality caused even by unjust means and to unjust men. Can you imagine that moment when Malchus locks eyes with the Savior as He replaces his severed ear? Jesus is kind!

> "And one of them struck the slave of the high priest and cut off his right ear. But Jesus answered and said, "Stop! No more of this." And He touched his ear and healed him"
>
> Luke 22:50-51

GOODNESS

The term 'Gospel' is translated as 'good news.' The Gospel is good news to all who hear and accept it. Jesus proclaimed the good news as He read from Isaiah 61 at the inauguration of His ministry. He is the Good Shepherd and He demonstrated the goodness of God everywhere He went and with all He came in contact with.

> "You know of Jesus of Nazareth, how God anointed Him with the Holy Spirit and with power, and how He went about doing good and

healing all who were oppressed by the devil, for God was with Him"

Acts 10:38

FAITHFULNESS

Jesus is faithful to God the Father and He is faithful to us. The Bible states why Jesus had to become a man like us:

> "This is why he had to be a Man and take hold of our humanity in every way. He made us his brothers and sisters and became our merciful and faithful King-Priest before God; as the One who removed our sins to make us one with Him"
>
> Hebrews 2:17 (TPT)

As Jesus remained faithful to God, fulfilling His mission to the cross, He was acting as our High Priest. He was faithful to His priestly calling. Jesus is faithful to us, despite our failings. Jesus never leaves us, although we leave Him. Peter, one of the most strong-willed disciples, boldly proclaims he will never leave Jesus, and hours later Peter denies Jesus with strong language. This brings Peter into the depths of despair when he realizes how he has treated Jesus. Jesus forgives and restores Peter. Jesus is faithful to us even when we are not faithful to Him.

GENTLENESS

Jesus, the King of Glory, humbled Himself to come to earth as a man. This fruit of the Spirit is called gentleness, which can also be translated as 'meek and humble.' Jesus called:

> "Come to Me, all who are weary and heavy-laden, and I will give you rest. Take My yoke upon you and learn from Me, for I am gentle and humble in heart, and you will find rest for your souls. For My yoke is easy and My burden is light"
>
> Matthew 11:28-30

Jesus states that we should learn from Him. Jesus is a strong King who is also gentle. He can minister to us in all of life's circumstances. The picture of a gentle Lord is one who gives us deep rest and does not throw heavy burdens on us. As we learn His ways, we find that He is easy to please and to walk with.

SELF-CONTROL

Jesus never acts in a self-serving manner. He lives to please His Father and carry out the Father's will. It is the model for a life that has the flesh in submission to the will of God. Even when faced with decisions that could impact the natural desires of the flesh, such as hunger and self-preservation, Jesus always chooses the higher way. We never observe Jesus in a moment of weakness, succumbing to temptation or reacting in a way out of alignment with His identity. When Jesus was being apprehended in the garden and His disciple resorts to physical force, Jesus tells him:

> "…or do you think that I cannot appeal to My Father, and He will at once put at My disposal more than twelve legions of angels? How then will the Scriptures be fulfilled, which say that it must happen this way?"
>
> Matthew 26:53

In the following 24 hours, Jesus will be beaten, mocked and whipped at the hands of powerful Roman guards whose life's purpose is to inflict pain on law breakers. Following this, He is put on full display in a humiliating, painful, torturous crucifixion. Yet through it all, He never steps out of submission to His Father's will.

COACHING

Do you see yourself in Paul's list, demonstrating examples of our self-life at the beginning of this chapter?

For whatever qualities you identify with from the 'self-life' list, identify a corresponding fruit of the Spirit that is needed in your life to replace your self-life craving.

- Love
- Joy
- Peace
- Patience
- Kindness
- Goodness
- Faithfulness
- Gentleness
- Self-Control

Pray that God shows you how to develop these qualities of the Spirit, and actively seek ways in which you can develop and demonstrate this fruit in your life.

Be aware – in my experience, when you pray for the manifestation of one of these qualities in your life, it does not instantly appear. The Lord may not make this desired quality immediately evident. It has been my experience that He allows us to have circumstances and to be in an environment that bring about what we ask for. If your prayer is for patience, you will not instantly get patience. You will get tested. Don't be surprised when situations arise that cause frustration, irritation and discontentment. View these situations as opportunities to develop and demonstrate patience.

"Many women were there looking on from a distance, who had followed Jesus from Galilee…"

———

Matthew 27:55a

JESUS LIBERATES WOMEN

JESUS STARTED THE WOMEN'S LIBERATION MOVEMENT

On the way from Judea to Galilee, Jesus takes the shortest route and cuts through Samaria, despite very strict, cultural barriers between the Jews and Samaritans. During this time in history, Samaritans were despised by Jews and were considered unclean. On this day at noon, Jesus sits by a well. As a Samaritan woman comes to draw water, Jesus engages her by asking her for a drink. Jesus is not only breaking the cultural norm of speaking with a Samaritan, He is speaking with a Samaritan woman. On top of that, He is alone with her at the well and is asking her for a drink, which would be forbidden because of her race.

As this woman came to draw water from the well, Jesus draws her in through His actions and engagement. He initiates a conversation, using the natural well to point to Himself as the spiritual living water. He stirs her curiosity as He speaks about the living water that He offers her leading to eternal life. Next, He confronts the sin in her life and reveals that He is the Messiah. He does not condemn her. It is His affectionate approach and focused interest into her life that draws her.

As a result of this encounter with Jesus, she leaves her water pot at the well and runs into her home city to announce:

> "'Come and meet a man at the well who told me everything I've ever done! He could be the Anointed One we've been waiting for.' Hearing this, the people came streaming out of the village to go see Jesus."
> John 4:29 (TPT)

Jesus breaks at least four social and cultural norms in this encounter.

1. He speaks to a despised race.
2. She is a woman.
3. She is alone.
4. He asks her for water.

In addition, Jesus was a Rabbi, which meant He was held to even stricter guidelines and etiquette, as He was forbidden to speak with a woman in public. Women were treated differently than men and were considered subservient in this time era.

The result of Jesus breaking with tradition led to a harvest within this Samaritan city.

> "So there were many from the Samaritan village who became believers in Jesus because of the woman's testimony: 'He told me everything I ever did!' Then they begged Jesus to stay with them, so he stayed there for two days, resulting in many more coming to faith in him because of his teachings. Then the Samaritans said to the woman, 'We no longer believe just because of what you told us, but now we've heard him ourselves and are convinced that he really is the true Savior of the world!'"
>
> John 4:39-42 (TPT)

Christians are often portrayed as repressive of women, forcing submission and condoning domination. This perspective is far from the truth and does not represent the freedom and equality Jesus brought to women. His approach was revolutionary and not without controversy in the day and time of His earthly ministry.

At the time Jesus lived, it was the culture for women to be treated differently than men. Consider just some of the cultural norms and deep routed traditions that Jesus shattered.

- At the beginning of His ministry His first miracle is manifested by His earthly mother's request. He honors her, and even though He plainly tells her it is not His time, He turns the water into wine.

- The Samaritan woman at the well: Jesus breaks at least four cultural norms in this exchange.

- The woman caught in the act of adultery: Jesus defends her, saves her from punishment, forgives her and admonishes her to go and sin no more (John 8:3-11).

- The woman who broke the alabaster box: Jesus defends her from the cutting comments and insults of the religious elite (Matthew 26:7 13).

- Jesus and the Syrophoenician woman: Jesus engages this gentile woman and grants her request by delivering her daughter from a demon (Mark 7:24-30, Matthew 15:22-28).

- He permitted women to travel with Him and be counted among the disciples (Luke 8:1-3).

- He first appears to a woman after His resurrection (John 20:11-18).

Jesus treats all women with respect and elevates their position within the culture. Through His interactions and interventions with women, He honors them despite the cultural and religious backlash. Jesus models real leadership and manhood by defending women throughout His life.

COACHING

Real men honor women. In today's culture, despite superficial equality, there persists an accepted culture of degrading and reducing women to lower status. This is evidenced at the extreme with the consumption in the billions of dollars of pornographic materials, stripping women of honor, esteem and identity. At more 'acceptable' levels, we see unprecedented numbers of women and young girls receiving a message through todays culture, television, movies and marketing that their value is found in their outward sex appeal. Social media channels are filled with girls seeking attention in an attempt to gather 'likes' and 'hearts.' In the Kingdom, God is no respecter of persons. He created male and female and we have distinct differences and unique qualities, but we are of equal value in the sight of our Creator.

THE PORN PANDEMIC

Some men believe that watching porn has no effect on themselves or society since it is done in secret. Science is now revealing the harmful effects of consuming pornography. From re-wiring your brain by forming new pathways through neuro-plasticity, to impacting your real-life relationships in a multitude of harmful ways. When you consume porn, you feed an industry that profits from the exploitation of women, potential sex slavery, pedophilia and human trafficking. The most efficacious way to combat this problem is by cutting off the consumption of porn in your life immediately, alerting other men to this pandemic and educating our children before they get ensnared.

Get educated and involved by visiting

www.fightthenewdrug.com

www.yourbrainonporn.com

"Blessed are the gentle, for they shall inherit the earth."

Matthew 5:5

JESUS IS GENTLE

Jesus is gentle. Picture Him playing with the children, kneeling down to their eye level, fixing His gaze in their direction. He is interested and full of love, and He engages these little ones with stories and His attention. Now see Him as a guest in Simon's home. Dinner is being served when the door flings open and an unknown woman forces her way in, falls at His feet, breaks open an expensive box filled with aromatic spices and anoints His feet, pouring out the costly oil mixture on His feet as she breaks down in worship in front of all present.

Jesus adapts His approach to each situation. Sometimes a harsh reply is warranted, but He never follows a rigid formula. When the woman with the costly perfume anoints Jesus' feet, the disciples were offended.

> "When the disciples saw this, they were offended. 'What a total waste!' they grumbled. 'We could have sold it for a great deal of money and given it to the poor.'"
>
> Matthew 26:8-9 (TPT)

Jesus, with His spiritual discernment and high level of E.Q., knows their thoughts and addresses them in a gentle way that corrects their error, guides them into a deeper truth and re-orders their internal values and priorities.

> "Jesus knew their thoughts and said to them, 'Why are you critical of this woman? She has done a beautiful act of kindness for me. You will always have someone poor whom you can help, but you will not always have me. When she poured the fragrant oil over me, she was preparing my body for burial. I promise you that as this wonderful gospel spreads all over the world, the story of her lavish devotion to me will also be mentioned in memory of her.'"
>
> Matthew 26:10-13

In this moment, Jesus is teaching how "devotion to Himself must precede and inform all other important and godly agendas" (IVP Bible Background Commentary, New Testament). This event was so important that it is to be shared in three of the Gospels.

GENTLENESS IS MEEKNESS

The word 'gentle' in the Bible is also interchangeable with the word 'meek.' We know that Jesus is described as 'meek' and proclaims, "The meek shall inherit the earth," during His famous Sermon on the Mount (Matthew 5:5). In our present culture's perception, men exhibiting traits seen as gentle is equal to being labeled as weak or timid. This is far from the truth, so let's take a closer look at the true meaning behind the word 'meek.'

> **Gentleness is meekness, and meekness is controlled power and strength**

We have already seen that Jesus is strong, passionate, outspoken and embraces confrontation; all characteristics diametrically opposed to weakness. So, how then do we interpret this word 'meek'? This is the best way I have heard this type of meekness described: 'power under control.' When Jesus entered earth's atmosphere taking on human flesh, He was still 100% God, but willingly made a choice to self-limit His power as Lord. In the Apostle Paul's letter to the Philippians, he writes, speaking of Jesus:

> "…but emptied Himself, taking the form of a bond-servant, and being made in the likeness of men. Being found in appearance as a man, He humbled Himself by becoming obedient to the point of death, even death on a cross."
>
> Philippians 2:7-8

This is the perfect picture of self-control and meekness. As Jesus stands before Pontus Pilate in a face-to-face meeting that will determine His future, He knows it will result in His death on a cross. Jesus stands there silent, choosing not to defend Himself. He fully embraces His mission and chooses to submit to His Father's will by standing in silence. This is ultimate strength; this is true power.

COACHING

How can we as men re-define and re-order the perceptions of true manhood? Jesus models strength under control as He exercised dominion over His emotions and the way He responds to everyone He comes in contact with. He is centered, controlled and steady. Today, men who attempt to display alpha characteristics focus on carrying themselves in a posture that projects outward strength. Maybe it is a look that intimidates, shields and hides the true, internal insecurities they hope to never reveal. This show of false strength is rooted in pride.

Gentleness and meekness are qualities of real strength operating under control and rooted in identity. Knowing who you are created to be and operating in your calling and purpose sets you free from seeking to shape how you are perceived by others. Jesus knows who He is and that's why He can be confident in being gentle and exhibiting meekness. Unlike the intimidating perception fake alphas try to exude, gentleness is welcoming and inviting.

"You should have the same attitude toward one another that Christ Jesus had, who though he existed in the form of God did not regard equality with God as something to be grasped, but emptied himself by taking on the form of a slave, by looking like other men, and by sharing in human nature. He humbled himself, by becoming obedient to the point of death - even death on a cross!"

Philippians 2:5-8 (TPT)

JESUS MODEL'S HUMILITY

We live in a day where the name of the game is getting attention. People are trying to find their leadership role by building platforms on social media and accumulating followers to secure a perceived leadership position. Attention has become the value system many are chasing, and with this pursuit there can be motivations of either hidden or overt pride. Jesus led the largest movement of His day with a spotlight of attention on Him everywhere He went. He is our model for humility, and as a leader He does not draw the attention to Himself. Isaiah prophesied the following about the Messiah:

> "The servant grew up before God—a scrawny seedling, a scrubby plant in a parched field. There was nothing attractive about him, nothing to cause us to take a second look. He was looked down on and passed over, a man who suffered, who knew pain firsthand."
> Isaiah 53:2-3 (MSG)

One of the hallmarks of a life that God is attracted to is humility. An abundance of scriptures state how the Lord is drawn to the lowly of heart and dwells with those of a broken and contrite spirit. God loves using the things considered low or of little value in the world's eyes to confound the logical, natural mind. From the way He chooses people, anoints kings and brings Jesus into His appointed time for humanity, we see a path of humility in those who are chosen and used in a mighty way for God. In Proverbs, we learn about seven things that God hates. The first listed is 'a proud look,' which is translated as 'putting others down while considering yourself superior' (Proverbs 6:16-17, TPT). It makes sense that since God explicitly states that He hates pride, He is attracted to humility. David writes:

> "For though you are lofty and exalted, you stoop to embrace the lowly. Yet you keep your distance from those filled with pride."
>
> Psalm 138:6 (TPT)

When addressing the crowds and the disciples in reference to the superficial spirituality of the religious scribes and Pharisees, Jesus states:

> "Whoever exalts himself shall be humbled; and whoever humbles himself shall be exalted."
>
> Matthew 23:12

These are not just mere words from Jesus. He lived this out by choosing the path of humility. When Jesus was preparing to make His entrance into Jerusalem, He gave the following instructions to His disciples:

> "Now, as they were approaching Jerusalem, they arrived at the place of the stables near Bethany on the Mount of Olives. Jesus sent two of his disciples ahead and said to them, 'As soon as you enter the village ahead, you will find a donkey's colt tethered there that has never been ridden. Untie it and bring it to me. And if anyone asks, 'Why are you taking it?' tell them, 'The master needs it and will send it back to you soon.' So they went and found the colt outside in the street, tied to a gate. When they started to untie it, some people standing there said to them, 'Why are untying that colt?' They answered just as Jesus had told them: 'The master needs it, and he will send it back to you soon.' So the bystanders let them go."
>
> Mark 11:1-6 (TPT)

His whole life is marked by ordinary surroundings, from blue-collar work to immersion into the culture of the working class. He chose to participate in life among the social ranks of the common people of the day. Even at this moment, on His way to embrace His destiny on a wooden cross, His choice of transportation is an ordinary work animal: a borrowed donkey. What makes this spectacular is the backdrop and tradition of kings in that time period. They would parade with great fanfare on horses and steeds upon entering the city. The very animal He chose to make His entrance on speaks of humility.

There are so many experiences, symbols and shadows found in the life of Jesus that speak to His humility. I have only highlighted a few here. Humility is a sign of great leadership just as demonstrating empathy is. Jesus does not use humility as a tactic. He is truly humble, and this trait marks His life, His leadership and how He relates to those He ministers to. He is our model for humility.

COACHING

As men, let's always keep an eye out for pride. We have a natural tendency to size each other up and find meaning in what we do and what we have. Financial status is the measuring rod for many men, and it can be easy to get pulled into pride around other guys. We must seek to find the balance between genuine humility and not being ashamed with what we have or do not have. The Bible states that godliness with contentment is great gain. The Apostle Paul learned how to abound with little and with much, may the same be said about us.

God opposes the proud (Proverbs 29:23, Luke 1:52, James 4:6, 1 Peter 5:5)

"Being deeply moved with tender compassion, Jesus reached out and touched the skin of the leper and told him, 'Of course I want you to be healed—so now, be cleansed!'"

Mark 1:41 (TPT)

JESUS IS A MAN OF COMPASSION

Jesus' experience as a man enables Him to be in tune with the deepest needs of humanity. He is keenly aware of His own emotions and tuned in to the emotions of those around Him. He is attentive, engaged and interested. Jesus presents a picture of the Father; a Father who is so attentive to us that it is hard to comprehend how the God of Heaven is interested in the smallest details of our lives. Jesus told His disciples that God is deeply interested and cares about the specifics of our life to such a level, even the hairs of our head are numbered (Matthew 10:29).

As a man, Jesus demonstrates genuine interest and care for those around Him. Some have over-spiritualized Jesus, claiming He is not interested in our physical well-being and that He is only concerned with the eternal. This is contrary to the Jesus of the Bible. Consider the catalyst for the feeding of the 4,000:

> "Jesus called his disciples to himself and said, 'I care deeply about all these people, for they've already been with me for three days without food. I don't want to send them away fasting or else they may be overcome by weakness on their journey home.'"
>
> Matthew 15:32 (TPT)

Here we see Jesus concerned with everything that affects humanity: both spiritual and physical needs concern Him and move Him to action. At another time, a man infected with leprosy calls out to Jesus, pleading for a physical healing. Here is this verse again:

> "Being deeply moved with tender compassion, Jesus reached out and touched the skin of the leper and told him, 'Of course I want you to be healed—so now, be cleansed!'"
>
> Mark 1:41 (TPT)

To be a leper at this time under Jewish law, meant to be quarantined from the public. It was forbidden to go near or touch those with leprosy. Despite this, Jesus is so concerned with this man's physical need that He does what was considered to be repulsive and physically touches the man. The Bible records that Jesus was deeply moved with compassion towards him. The word 'compassion' in the original language describes an 'intense emotion and deep yearning.' If Jesus was only concerned with the spiritual condition of this man, there would be no need for physical healing. Instead, we see Jesus acting in alignment with His emotion towards this man's circumstance.

THE WIDOW OF NAIN

One day, Jesus came across a funeral procession for a young man whose mother was a widow. As soon as Jesus laid eyes on this distraught woman full of grief, the Bible records that He felt compassion for her and initiated a conversation by saying, "Please don't cry." Jesus proceeds to the casket, declares life to the boy and he instantly sits up and speaks. His action of compassion not only brings healing to the hurting and restores family, He draws people into relationship with God. The Bible describes the sense of awe that struck the crowd as the atmosphere of resurrection power is manifested among them. As a result, the people began to worship and glorify God (Luke 7:16).

Compassion draws people to Jesus

The life of Jesus was marked with compassion for people. We could say compassion compelled Him to minister to the needs of those around Him. While He is in the height of His ministry, traveling and performing miracles to meet the physical needs of those around Him, we read the following as seen through the eyes of Matthew:

> "Jesus was going through all the cities and villages, teaching in their synagogues and proclaiming the gospel of the kingdom, and healing every kind of disease and every kind of sickness. Seeing the people,

He felt compassion for them, because they were distressed and dispirited like sheep without a shepherd. Then He said to His disciples, 'The harvest is plentiful, but the workers are few. Therefore beseech the Lord of the harvest to send out workers into His harvest.'"
Matthew 9:35-38

Here we see the compassion of Jesus noted again in connection with His heart for shepherding people in their broken condition. The immediate request of Jesus is to pray for more workers to be sent into the harvest with the same heart for ministry that He has. Men, Jesus needs you and I to pick up this burden, see the present-day condition of those around us and out of compassion and a love for the lost, take action to be counted as a worker in the Lord's Harvest.

COACHING

You are called to be a leader whether you have a title or not. In our quest to influence others and grow in our leadership capacity, we must be on guard to always check our internal motives and the condition of our heart. Some men want to influence and impact others for the need it fills within themselves. The need to be valued, the need to be recognized, the need to be heard. We are to get our self-worth from our identity as sons of God, not the title, position or influence we exert. Jesus leads with a heart of compassion; it is the driving force that fuels His actions and it must be ours as well. Jesus sees a need and is moved to action with a pure motivation. Compassion compels Him to act.

We are called to leadership and must first lead ourselves. It is easy to become self-absorbed, only focused on our world and the issues that directly impact us. Many men live glued to their screens, numb to the people and circumstances around them. This self-centered perspective can leave us disconnected from the situations and opportunities where we can demonstrate compassion. Compassion draws people to Jesus.

"But if anyone abuses one of these little ones who believe in me, it would be better for him to have a heavy boulder tied around his neck and be hurled into the deepest sea than to face the punishment he deserves!"

Matthew 18:6 (TPT)

JESUS DEFENDS THE WEAK

Imagine you have been lame for 38 years, unable to walk, work or contribute to society in any meaningful way. You find yourself lying on a mat in a public courtyard with hundreds of others who are suffering in similar conditions. Your dreams and aspirations are dead. You have a hope that one day you may be healed, but that day has never come. This day, however is different. A man approaches you and poses this question:

"Do you really want to be healed?"

Conditioned to have a low expectation you point to the impossibility of your situation. This man suddenly and with strong conviction declares a command: "Stand up! Pick up your mat and you will walk!"

There is something about His voice, His boldness and strength balanced with a compassion you have never encountered. Your visceral response is to stand despite the atrophy from not using your legs for almost four decades. Strength fills your lower limbs as the impossible is manifesting within your body. Flooded with love, faith and new-found strength, you obey the command and roll up your mat and place one foot in front of the other in a rhythm that you thought you had forgotten.

You turn around, but the healer is no longer there. In His place is the stern gaze of men in long black robes with judgement in their eyes, angrily demanding to know what happened and berating you for holding your mat. You don't have the answers. Later you meet Jesus, who lovingly admonishes you to sin no more.

This is the account of the lame man found in John chapter five. What happens next is a powerful picture of Jesus as our defender. After being healed, the (former) lame man was questioned by the religious order for carrying his bed on the Sabbath. After an interaction with Jesus, he tells the Pharisees that it was Jesus who healed him and instructed him to pick up his bed and walk on this day. Jesus firmly addresses the Pharisees, speaking of His relationship with His Father and His mission. While this is occurring, imagine the man who was just healed, watching as he stands among a captivated crowd. This man would realize Jesus is taking on the Pharisees to shield him. Jesus is a powerful man who defends what is right, He is honorable and He stands up for the weak.

CORBAN

Jesus cares and is concerned with our everyday needs. On one occasion, Jesus strongly rebuked the religious leaders for instructing people that it was approved to reallocate money that was earmarked to support their aging parents and declare it as a holy offering to God.

> "...but you say, 'If a man says to his father or his mother, whatever I have that would help you is Corban (that is to say, given to God),' you no longer permit him to do anything for his father or his mother.'"
> Mark 7:11

The Pharisees gladly enforced this practice of accepting this money as offerings. Jesus rebukes them for violating the spirit of the law and looking for loopholes. Why was He so concerned about ensuring this money went to the elderly? It is driven by His compassion and attention to physical, natural needs. Here we see Jesus defending the weak once again, concerned with their welfare and earthly condition. He stands up for honor and breaks with tradition. It makes me wonder how long Jesus pondered this topic. Did He hear of someone this happened to? Did He hear directly from parents who financial support was withheld from?

In any case, Jesus is a fierce defender of the innocent. We see this with the consequence He references for anyone who abuses a child, as well as the care and honoring of the elderly among us. He brings the unjust practices of the day to the forefront and addresses them head on, not shying away from confrontation.

COACHING

Jesus shows us that real men stand up and defend the innocent and defenseless. In this chapter, we examined how Jesus treats everyone with value despite their physical limitations or condition. He looks out for the poor, stands up for the elderly and defends children. He also serves as a voice that stands up to injustice. When the Pharisees attack His disciples, He responds in their defense:

> "If only you could learn the meaning of the words 'I want compassion more than a sacrifice,' you wouldn't be condemning my innocent disciples."
>
> Matthew 12:7 (TPT)

Jesus is our model of a strong, good man.

When it comes to children, the verse quoted at the beginning of this chapter demonstrates Jesus' fierce commitment to innocent little ones. One practical way that my family and I have sought to aid children is by sponsoring children through Compassion International. Each of our children have a child they sponsor and correspond with. It keeps them grounded and in touch with how privileged we are here in America, while supporting others with the Gospel message and helping to meet their physical and educational needs. If you're interested in learning more, you can visit:

https://www.compassion.com

"'Which is easier, to say, 'Your sins are forgiven,' or to say, 'Get up, and walk'? But so that you may know that the Son of Man has authority on earth to forgive sins'—then He said to the paralytic, 'Get up, pick up your bed and go home.'"

Matthew 9:5-6

JESUS FORGIVES AND RESTORES

When we look at the original purpose of man as identified in Genesis, man was to be an heir and king of the earth, managing, ruling and reigning over God's creation in a highly-esteemed role. We even read in Hebrews and Psalms that man was created just a little lower than the angels (Psalms 8:5, Hebrews 2:7). Our rightful position of king of the earth was forfeited through the sin of Adam. Jesus came to reconcile us back to the Father and into our proper position as a joint heir within the Kingdom of God (Romans 8). It is with this backdrop that we can view Jesus as the true Redeemer who came to restore us back into alignment with our Father.

Jesus has eyes to see beyond the actions of people into their brokenness, past and into their soul. Why did Jesus come? To offer Himself as a sacrifice, so that we would be forgiven and reconciled to God. Jesus says of Himself:

> "For the Son of Man has come to seek and to save that which was lost."
>
> Luke 19:10

After Jesus healed those with diseases in the Gospel accounts, He offered them forgiveness and directed them to, "Go and sin no more." In John 5, after Jesus heals the man at the pool of Bethesda, His instruction is the same.

> "Behold, you have become well; do not sin anymore, so that nothing worse happens to you."
>
> John 5:14 (TPT)

What did Jesus do when He crossed paths with the Pharisees who brought a woman caught in the act of adultery and angrily demanded to know what they should do with her? Quoting the Old Testament law, they knew that they had the right to stone her. Jesus diffused the situation, masterfully directing their attention to the sin in their own lives and heals and restores this woman by stating:

> "'Woman, where are they? Did no one condemn you?' She said, 'No one, Lord.' And Jesus said, 'I do not condemn you, either. Go. From now on sin no more.'"
>
> John 8:11

PETER THE ROCK

One of the greatest accounts we have of forgiveness and restoration is that of Peter. Peter was viewed as the leader of the 12 disciples. He certainly acted as spokesman and is known for his head-first approach in following Jesus. His personality was strong and unique – the only disciple to request to walk on water with the Master and the one who literally grabbed Jesus, pulled Him aside and rebuked the Lord for prophesying that He would be put to death. Throughout the Gospels, Peter is unashamed and seemingly willing to go to great lengths to support Jesus.

At a gathering of the 12 around Jesus after the last Passover, Peter again pledges his allegiance to Jesus, stating:

> "Even though all may fall away because of You, I will never fall away."
>
> Matthew 26:33

Jesus responds to Peter by stating:

> "'Truly I say to you that this very night, before a rooster crows, you will deny Me three times.' Peter *said to Him, 'Even if I have to die with You, I will not deny You.' All the disciples said the same thing too."
>
> Matthew 26:34-35

It was true. Later that same evening, Peter denies even knowing Jesus with the use of strong language to a woman who questioned him. This throws Peter into the depths of despair after realizing what he had done. Jesus was not only his Lord, but also his friend. They spent years with each other, traveling, ministering, laughing and sharing life together. In one moment, Peter felt as though it all evaporated as he forsook Jesus.

Jesus will forgive Peter, and later appears to Him after His resurrection. Peter's relationship with Jesus is fully restored, and Jesus installs Him into the office of Apostle. This is the ultimate picture of full restoration as Peter becomes the Apostle to the Jews, and later in life, he will be put to death for his allegiance to Jesus. At Peter's death he requests to be crucified upside down, counting himself unworthy to die in the same manner as Jesus.

COACHING

The first step as we enter our Christian walk is repenting and asking for forgiveness. We are called to regularly examine ourselves and our hearts to ensure we are walking in right standing with the Lord. Part of the Apostle Paul's charge to the church before participating in communion is to examine ourselves.

> "But a man must examine himself, and in so doing he is to eat of the bread and drink of the cup."
>
> 1 Corinthians 11:28

After repenting and accepting the Lord's forgiveness in our own lives, next is to ensure there is no unforgiveness in our lives towards others, regardless of how they may have wronged us. The best analogy I have heard regarding unforgiveness is, "Harboring unforgiveness is like drinking poison and expecting the other person to die." Scientific research reveals the harmful effects of harboring toxic emotions, like unforgiveness can have on our health. Many people wrestle with forgiving people who have taken advantage, harmed or wronged them. However, we have clear instructions: be like Jesus and forgive. If this is you, don't put it off. Do it today.

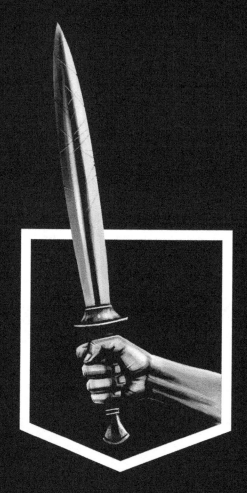

Book V
Confrontation

THE SWORD

THE SWORD

JESUS IS A MAN OF TRUTH

JESUS IS A MAN OF COURAGE

JESUS IS A MAN OF ENDURANCE

JESUS IS A MAN OF CONFRONTATION

JESUS PROVIDES CORRECTION

JESUS IS DISCERNING OF MAN

JESUS IS NOT SAFE

JESUS IS A MAN OF PURPOSE AND PASSION

"Do not think that I came to bring peace on the earth; I did not come to bring peace, but a sword."

Matthew 10:34

THE SWORD

Jesus was a revolutionary. He ushered in a new era for all of humanity, and the way we relate to God will never be the same. The people of Israel expected a warring Messiah coming to liberate them from the bondage of Rome. Jesus is the Deliverer, and He does enter into conflict and bring freedom to captives, but not in the way the nation of Israel expected at the time. The battle He wages and the sword He wields is in the spiritual realm. One of His titles and names is 'Prince of Peace.' John captures the moment when, before Jesus departs the disciples, He states that, "Peace I leave with you; My peace I give to you…" (John 14:27). The mission of Jesus was to restore peace between man and God. That peace is offered to those who respond to the message of the Gospel with repentance. For those who do not, there will be no peace. Jesus plainly stated:

> "Perhaps you think I've come to spread peace and calm over the earth—but my coming will bring conflict and division, not peace. Because of me, a son will turn against his father, a daughter her mother and against her mother-in-law. Within your own families you will find enemies.
>
> Matthew 10:34-36 (TPT)

He is telling His disciples that being His follower brings them into a battle with the world and its systems. Jesus also warned His disciples:

> "Just remember, when the unbelieving world hates you, they first hated me. If you were to give your allegiance to the world, they would love and welcome you as one of their own. But because you won't align yourself with the values of this world, they will hate you."
>
> John 15:18-19 (TPT)

Jesus paints a vivid picture of the true cost of being a disciple: rejection, suffering and conflict. Jesus wields a sword and leads us in battle, but the battle is not against people or nations as the world understands a revolution. It is against the unseen forces in the spiritual realm, which control this world and its systems. The Apostle Paul states it this way:

> "For we do not wrestle against flesh and blood, but against principalities, against powers, against the rulers of the darkness of this age, against spiritual hosts of wickedness in the heavenly places."
>
> Ephesians 6:12 (NKJV)

The Apostle John, who walked with Jesus as a teenager, writes the following over 60 years later:

> "The Son of God appeared for this purpose, to destroy the works of the devil."
>
> 1 John 3:8b

Yes brothers, we are in a fight. We are born into a battle and the One we follow carries a sword.

"…I am the Way,
I am the Truth,
and I am the Life…"

———

John 14:6

JESUS IS A MAN OF TRUTH

At the illegal midnight trial, out of the view of the public, the Sanhedrin (the religious governing order) abuse Jesus and bring Him in for questioning. They argue with themselves over 'hear say' and they can't get their stories straight. The witnesses will not agree. Their shoddy case is disintegrating before their eyes and their evil intentions are surfacing in plain sight. In this moment, Jesus does not seek to defend Himself. He certainly could have, but He is in submission to the will of His Father. Despite no wrong doing, He willfully lays down His ability to dismantle their weak attempts to ensnare Him in a violation of the Jewish laws (Mark 14). Finally, Chief Priest Caiaphas asks Jesus directly:

> "Are you the anointed Messiah, the Son of the Blessed God?"

Jesus responds:

> "I am. And more than that, you are about to see the Son of Man seated at the right hand of the Almighty and coming in the heavenly clouds!"
>
> Mark 14:61b-62 (TPT)

It is at this point outrage erupts. The High Priest tears His garments and a beating of a blindfolded Jesus ensues along with a guilty verdict (Mark 14:63-65). Jesus is a man of truth; He is truth and cannot lie. He is fearless in the face of His accusers even when they possess earthly advantage over Him. He is rock solid in in His purpose and identity, never forfeiting His call even in His weakest moment. As Jesus faces a death sentence in the hands of the Roman Governor, Pontus Pilate, He owns His identity.

> "Therefore Pilate said to Him, 'So You are a king?' Jesus answered, 'You say correctly that I am a king. For this I have been born, and for this I have come into the world, to testify to the truth. Everyone who is of the truth hears My voice.'"
>
> John 18:37

Truth is a person; Jesus is truth. He proclaimed:

> "…I am the way, and the truth, and the life; no one comes to the Father but through Me."
>
> John 14:6

One of the most common images people fashion of Jesus for themselves is a peaceful, hippie-like leader who only carries a message of love. This can inaccurately paint an image of a man on a mission preaching love and acceptance, never challenging, correcting or ever offending. The Gospel says His message is offensive.

> "For the word of the cross is foolishness to those who are perishing, but to us who are being saved it is the power of God."
>
> 1 Corinthians 1:18

> "'…The stone which the builders rejected, this became the very corner stone,' and, 'A stone of stumbling and A rock of offense'; for they stumble because they are disobedient to the word, and to this doom they were also appointed."
>
> 1 Peter 2:7-8

The truth can be offensive and as we will examine, Jesus speaks truth with no regard to the feelings of the hearers. This does not mean that He is intentionally offensive. Truth itself can be offensive; the Gospel is an offense. For example, if you are not walking in truth, when you are confronted with the truth you may be offended. Despite the emotional response and hurt feelings of those who are challenged with the truth, Jesus knows and teaches that the truth will set people free. It is the ultimate act of love to speak truth into a situation, bringing light and life where there is darkness and error.

If someone's house is on fire and they do not realize it, love for the truth will compel you to tell them, regardless of whether they agree, hold the same beliefs or will be offended. Jesus unabashedly does the hard thing, always bringing truth to every situation He encounters that needs correction.

We are not to be intentionally offensive in our attempt to bring truth. The Gospel truth itself, is an offense to some. Instead, we should speak the truth in love to bring correction where it is needed.

COACHING

Our seeker-sensitive culture has almost made it taboo to speak the truth about open sin in others' lives. Truth confronts and truth sets others free. The difference between wielding truth as a weapon of destruction or one of restoration is motive and relationship. When truth is shared because of a relationship with pure intentions and the intent is to set someone free, it can bring correction that may save someone from massive damage. I encourage you to pray about where God has placed you, who you are in relationship with and where you can bring truth to situations at home, in the workplace or with a friend.

"…Be brave and don't be afraid. I am here!"

Matthew 14:27 (TPT)

JESUS IS A MAN OF COURAGE

JESUS IS RELENTLESSLY FEARLESS

"On another Sabbath day, Jesus was teaching in the synagogue. In the room with him was a man with a deformed right hand. Everyone watched Jesus closely, especially the Jewish religious leaders and the religious scholars, to see if Jesus would heal on a Sabbath day, for they were eager to find a reason to accuse him of breaking the Jewish laws. Jesus, knowing their every thought, said to the man with the deformed hand, 'Come and stand here in the middle of the room.' So he got up and came forward. Jesus said to all who were there, 'Let me ask you a question. Which is better: to heal or to do harm on the Sabbath day? I have come to save a life, but you have come to find a life to destroy.' One by one Jesus looked into the eyes of each person in the room. Then he said to the man, 'Stretch out your arm and open your hand!' With everyone watching intently, he stretched out his arm, and his hand was completely healed! The room erupted with bitter rage because of this Sabbath-day healing. And from that moment on, the religious leaders plotted among themselves about how they might harm Jesus."

Luke 6:6-11 (TPT)

Jesus was not an appeaser; He never went along to get along. He did the hard thing; the thing that was inconvenient, the thing that was challenging and confrontative. He was a real man and model of courage, challenging the status quo and in-the-box thinking.

In this synagogue scene, the man with the deformed hand stands in full gaze of the onlooking crowd. This man most likely went through his entire life with a deformity that caused embarrassment and whispers everywhere he went. Some may have thought he sinned or perhaps his parents sinned. He is forced to carry the shame and weakness associated with a man who suffers from a deformity in that time period.

Jesus steps up in front of the crowds and makes direct eye contact with everyone in the room to ensure they were listening and watching. He then openly defies their opinions, and the man is instantly healed. This was most definitely a dramatic moment. The atmosphere was so charged with hate against Him, that they literally erupted with rage after He healed the man.

This gives us a model for overcoming those who would try to intimidate with their opinions, self-righteousness, religiousness and accusations. Isn't that exactly what the enemy does today? The most conflict comes before a mighty work. It is as if the enemy knows the power is about to be released, so he wields every weapon to silence Jesus, just as he attempts to do to us.

Jesus is brave. He knew where He was going and He knew where He was leading His team. After He discloses what will happen to Him when He goes to Jerusalem, the disciples cannot believe that any man would choose to walk into a pre-set trap. The actions of Jesus defy the logic of men. Just look at their reaction to Jesus when He willingly, knowingly walks into the fire and embraced the cross set before Him.

> "Jesus and his disciples were on the road that went up to Jerusalem, and Jesus was leading them forward. The disciples were filled with wonder and amazement at his bravery, but those following along with them were very afraid. As they approached the city, he took the Twelve aside privately and told them what was going to happen. 'I want you to know that we are going to Jerusalem, where the Son of Man will be handed over to the ruling priests and religious scholars and they will condemn him to death and hand him over to the Romans. And they will mock him, spit in his face, torture him, and kill him, but three days later he will rise again.'"
>
> Mark 10:32-34 (TPT)

The most conflict comes immediately before a mighty work

Later on, just outside Jerusalem's city walls, Jesus has walked with eleven of His disciples to the Garden of Gethsemane. The Roman mob, led by Judas the betrayer, approaches in darkness to apprehend Jesus. Jesus stands up and addresses this gang of Roman soldiers, still breathing heavy from rushing into the garden on a manhunt with swords and clubs in hand. Jesus displays His courage again as He allows Himself to be captured as part of God's prophetic plan. He submits to their unjust plot, but He does not lie down like a mute lamb. He stands up to the heavily armed Roman unit of soldiers with the religious order looking on. Jesus calls them out for their cowardly action of arresting Him in the dark of night when they had every opportunity to make their move in public daylight (Matt 26:55).

> "What is this—coming out after me with swords and clubs as if I were a dangerous criminal? Day after day I have been sitting in the Temple teaching, and you never so much as lifted a hand against me."
> Matthew 26:55 (MSG)

JESUS IS COURAGEOUS.

COACHING

THE FEAR OF MAN

As men, we have been conditioned to play our positions within society. The minute we get inspired and attempt to move forward with an act that requires courage, the enemy steps up to remind us why we will fail. "You're not enough for this." "You've failed before." "What will they think?"

What is the dream you have been harboring in your heart? Can you connect the fear of launching out with the enemy's plan to silence you? Jesus came to give us the abundant life and peace unlike the world has ever known. Abundance and peace are the opposites of living a life within the boundaries of fear.

For years I lived in fear, afraid of losing what I had gained in material wealth. As a husband and father, I walked under the pressure to provide for my family. Although I worked in an above-average career, I was fearful of what would happen if I lost my job. I would game plan various scenarios, thinking of ways we could survive if I was downsized. My mindset was truly one of scarcity. Jesus delivered me from that way of thinking and showed me how 'man' is not my source of provision. He shifted me into the mindset of heaven, the abundant mindset, knowing that all that I have is from my Father in heaven. It may be delivered through earthly means, but He is my true source. No one or no circumstance can cut me off from my Father's will to provide, bless and meet my every need.

"fixing our eyes on Jesus, the author and perfecter of faith, who for the joy set before Him endured the cross, despising the shame, and has sat down at the right hand of the throne of God."

Hebrews 12:2

JESUS IS A MAN OF ENDURANCE

The night in the Garden of Gethsemane is one of the most ominous, heart-wrenching accounts we have of our Lord. Jesus in agony, wrestling in prayer before going to the cross. Jesus knows His destiny; He has walked out His Father's will perfectly. All of the dominos are falling into place. In the time leading up to His final days before His crucifixion, He has set all things in order (from words of knowledge regarding the Passover location to His final meal with His disciples and warning of betrayal). He leads His close-knit tribe to the garden commonly known as 'the oil press.' He tells His disciples to watch and pray. He moves deeper into seclusion within the garden and takes Peter, James and John and provides the same instruction: "watch and pray" (Matthew 26:41).

The Gospel account of what happens next paints a gut-wrenching and heartbreaking scene of Jesus in extreme emotional stress. He is literally on the edge of pre-mature death, knowing all that will transpire in the next 24 hours. He calls upon His Father to sustain Him until the appointed time, so that He may accomplish all that He has come to do. This night of stress induced a condition where He sweats drops of blood, a rare condition called Hematidrosis, where one's sweat will contain blood. Medical science shows that the sweat glands are surrounded by tiny blood vessels. These vessels can constrict and then dilate to the point of rupture, causing blood to effuse into the sweat glands. Its cause? Extreme anguish. You can read more about it here: www.gotquestions.org/sweat-blood-Jesus.html

Jesus was never needy. He served His crew as an unwavering leader, a consistent leader, exhibited servanthood and humility, a man of fearless strength and stature. This night, in His greatest hour of need, He could use the support of His closest friends. He had one request of the men He spent the last three years of His life with. His ask was watch and pray with me.

Jesus never placed His trust in human flesh, knowing that we are weak and will fail in our frailty. In our flesh and natural state, we are feeble and weak. Three times during this hour Jesus goes back to His friends and asks them to continue to pray. Three times He finds them sleeping, unable to keep their eyes open during this historical moment. The third time Jesus exclaims:

> "Do you plan on sleeping and resting indefinitely? That's enough sleep! The end has come and the hour has arrived for the Son of Man to be handed over to the authority of sinful men. Get up and let's go. Don't you see? My betrayer draws near."
>
> Mark 14:41-42 (TPT)

In a single moment, Judas appears with a gang of heavily armed men. A kiss is given, moves are made, aggression is the response of Peter, and healing is provided by Jesus (in an attempt to defend Jesus, Peter unsheathes a sword and cuts off the high priest's servant's ear. Jesus rebukes Peter and heals the man's ear).

Consider the moments leading up to this violent confrontation in the garden, Jesus moves from an emotionally exhausted state to one of fearlessness in the face of violent men. While He confidently and securely confronts the angry mob, His disciples sprint into the distance. Hearts beating, adrenaline pumping and breath burning in their lungs, they all take off in different directions without looking back, fleeing from the one they referred to as Master and pledged their allegiance to.

See Jesus standing there alone – three years of friendship, spiritual encounters and some of the greatest shared experiences ever recorded in the pages of this world's history evaporated in a moment. Like a gun fired at the start of a race, His disciples have fled. Jesus is unmoved, He is unflinching in the face of His accusers. He is brave; He exhibits fearlessness, boundless courage and endures injustice and cruelty for the prize set before Him.

Jesus calls upon us to run our race with endurance. The writer of Hebrews states the following:

> "Therefore, since we have so great a cloud of witnesses surrounding us, let us also lay aside every encumbrance and the sin which so easily entangles us, and let us run with endurance the race that is set before us, fixing our eyes on Jesus, the author and perfecter of faith, who for the joy set before Him endured the cross, despising the shame, and has sat down at the right hand of the throne of God. For consider Him who has endured such hostility by sinners against Himself, so that you will not grow weary and lose heart."
> Hebrews 12:1-3

THE PHYSICAL ENDURANCE OF JESUS

We looked at the spiritual endurance of Jesus and in light of the physical hardships and torture He undergoes, it is also important to point out His physical endurance. Jesus was a good steward of everything, including His physical temple – His body. The discipline He developed encompassed every area of His life, not only the spiritual realm. There is no doubt that Jesus was a physically-strong man.

Working a blue-collar business for the majority of His earthly life, consuming a Middle Eastern diet, incorporating fasting as part of His routine and traveling long distances by foot leaves little question that Jesus was in great physical shape. These lifestyle choices and His daily disciplines gives Him the physical capacity to pull Peter out of the water, pray all night while everyone else is asleep, as well as flip tables and forcibly throw out all the merchants who were selling goods within the temple. Jesus possesses the internal strength and will to endure a Roman scourging and then refuse the painkiller cocktail of wine and gall He is offered while hanging on the cross in pain and physical agony.

COACHING

Just as we need to build endurance and capacity in our natural life and physical body, we need spiritual conditioning to go the distance in the areas we are called to by the Lord. We can do this by dedicating ourselves to daily disciplines that strengthen our spirit man. Endurance is about building our capacity to run faster, go farther and be stronger. Just as an athlete trains to build their physical endurance, we must train spiritually to go the distance and reach our full potential. Our spiritual training and nutrition can come in a number of forms. Two ways we can train and nourish our spirit man to grow to full capacity are through meditating on the Word of God and prayer.

"…You are also hopeless frauds, you experts of the law! For you crush people beneath the burden of obeying impossible religious regulations, yet you would never even think of doing them yourselves. What hypocrites!"

Luke 11:46 (TPT)

JESUS IS A MAN OF CONFRONTATION

We know Jesus is a man of truth, and sometimes speaking the truth can require you to be confrontative. In one interaction, the Pharisees approach Jesus with a question, attempting to ensnare Him, and they acknowledge that He speaks the truth without regard to the consequences.

> "So they approached him and said, 'Teacher, we know that you're an honest man of integrity and you teach us the truth of God's ways. We can clearly see that you're not one who speaks only to win the people's favor, because you speak the truth without regard to the consequences. So tell us, then, what you think. Is it proper for us to pay taxes to Caesar or not?'"
>
> Mark 12:14 (TPT)

> **Jesus speaks the truth without regard to consequences**

JESUS WARNS AGAINST THE RELIGIOUS SCHOLARS

Jesus does not back down or shy away from a confrontation, He never compromises what is true. During this same interaction Jesus gives a warning to the people about the religious leaders while in their presence. In full public display Jesus offers a strong warning about the hypocritical behavior of the religious scholars, speaking directly to their greed, lust for power and recognition.

> "Jesus also taught the people, 'Beware of the religious scholars. They love to parade around in their clergy robes and be greeted with respect on the street. They crave to be made the leaders of synagogue councils, and they push their way to the head table at banquets. For

appearance's sake, they will pray long religious prayers at the homes of widows for an offering, cheating them out of their very livelihood. Beware of them all, for they will one day be stripped of honor, and the judgment they receive will be severe.'"

Mark 12:38-40 (TPT)

In this passage, Jesus gives a warning to the people about the religious leaders…while in their presence. Confrontation! We have multiple accounts of Jesus issuing scathing criticism of the religious Pharisees, taking them to task in the open air where the public can look on and hear the injustice and sinfulness of these so-called religious men. In the famous account found in Luke 11, Jesus calls these religious leaders hypocrites and goes on to list specific examples of their greed and pride. He addresses these issues where all can see and hear, and He is unrelenting in His approach. He will not be intimidated to back down. As He is issuing this rebuke, He hears the following response:

> "Just then a specialist in interpreting religious law blurted out, "But Teacher, don't you realize that your words insult me and those of my profession? You're being rude to us all!"

Luke 11:45 (TPT)

Jesus confronts injustices and stands up for the weak. As Christian men in the Kingdom, the code of righteousness is imprinted upon our hearts. We are called to stand up, confront injustice and defend the defenseless. There is a code of honor in the Kingdom that drives us to protect and provide for those who need assistance. Jesus models this behavior in a way that attacks the very foundation of a corrupt religious political system; a system that seeks to ensnare the ones it was called to serve, but has now profited from the poor.

As men in the Kingdom, we do not run away from hard situations; we are called to confront.

Jesus is more obsessed with truth than concerned with offending those who hear it

COACHING

Men today no longer face the type of situations Jesus encountered. This does not alleviate us from the responsibility of confronting injustice and ministering freedom to the defenseless when opportunities arise.

HERE ARE A FEW WAYS THAT WE CAN MAKE AN IMPACT:

- Go on a mission trip to assist the poor and defenseless.
- Start your own initiative.
- Commit to pray for these issues.
- Provide time or money to organizations that invest in these causes.
- Voice of the Martyrs: https://www.persecution.com

ORGANIZATIONS THAT SUPPORT, FEED AND EDUCATE CHILDREN

- https://www.stopfortheone.org
- https://www.samaritanspurse.org
- https://www.worldvision.org

ORGANIZATIONS THAT FIGHT HUMAN TRAFFICKING

- https://www.a21.org
- https://ourrescue.org
- https://www.ijm.org/
- https://www.notforsalecampaign.org
- https://www.hookersforjesus.net

"Get behind Me, Satan; for you are not setting your mind on God's interests, but man's."

———

Mark 8:33b

JESUS PROVIDES CORRECTION

You may have heard it said that feedback is a gift. Receiving feedback helps us identify blind spots. We all have opportunity areas that need adjustment. When we are made aware of something that is hindering us, we have the opportunity to respond and course correct, setting us on a trajectory of success. At times, more intense correction is needed; more intense than just listening to the feedback of a coach. When you need to correct bad behavior in your children, coaching them to understand is not always the answer. Some situations need to be acknowledged and attitudes need to be adjusted with stern correction.

Jesus has the courage and love to provide correction. Some men struggle with receiving correction and can have a hard time showing humility and being teachable. Ultimately, correction is a display of love. Jesus loves you enough to not leave you in error. Jesus loves you enough that He wants you to experience life abundantly. We cannot have the full experience of abundant life if we reject adjustments and do not have a teachable spirit, willing to accept correction even when it hurts.

THE DISCIPLES CANNOT CAST OUT A DEMON

Jesus adapts His approach in the way He offers correction. At times a gentle touch is needed, and at other times the correction comes in the form of a stern rebuke. Jesus does not hold back, water it down or sugar coat His correction. When talking with the man who brought his demon-possessed son to Jesus for deliverance, the man shared with Jesus that he first went to the disciples and gives the report that they were ineffective in their ministry.

"Jesus said to the crowd, "Why are you such a faithless people? How much longer must I remain with you and put up with your unbelief? Now, bring the boy to me."

Mark 9:19 (TPT)

WHAT A WASTE

When the woman barged in the room when Jesus was having a private dinner at Simon's house and broke open her precious alabaster box of costly perfume and poured the anointing mixture onto Jesus' feet, pious and proud looks filled the house. Comments erupted that this was a total waste and wholly inappropriate. The religious spirit scolded the woman who was engaged in an act of true worship. They attempted to minimize her worship and place her in the confines of a box. They deemed her act as an unacceptable way to address Jesus.

They cloaked their comments in false piety that the money could have been given to the poor. Jesus defies them and defends her when He comments that the poor will always be here and you can help them whenever you like. He exposes their false intentions towards the poor. He justifies her and then pronounces a memorial over her lavish act of worship, it will be recorded and retold forever. Jesus is instituting the culture of honor. He is willing to accept praise and does not exhibit a false humility that displaces the honor that she is giving Him (Mark 14:6-9). The disciples are in error, and Jesus brings the correction to re-order their thinking and change the course of their dialogue.

JESUS REBUKES AND CORRECTS

On another occasion, Jesus was warning His disciples about the hypocrisy of the Pharisees and Sadducees. The disciples who misinterpret Jesus' discourse with them think He is speaking about the fact that they forgot to bring bread with them on their trip. Look at how Jesus responds:

"Knowing their thoughts, Jesus said to them, 'You have such little faith! Why are you arguing with one another about having no bread? Are you so slow to understand?'"

Matt 16:8-9a (TPT)

Jesus accuses the disciples of being slow to 'get it' when they don't immediately recognize what He is referring to. The correction given here is meant to ground them in God's power to provide, and then He goes on to tell them who His original comment was regarding.

PETER'S REBUKE

When Peter declares that Jesus is the Christ, the promised Messiah, Jesus warns the 12 to tell no one what they are all now aware of. The account unfolds with Jesus openly discussing what must happen to the 'Son of Man.'

> "And He began to teach them that the Son of Man must suffer many things and be rejected by the elders and the chief priests and the scribes, and be killed, and after three days rise again."
>
> Mark 8:31

After hearing these things, Peter ('The Rock') with his stubborn will and earthly motivation, actually starts rebuking the one he has just declared as Messiah!

> "And He was stating the matter plainly. And Peter took Him aside and began to rebuke Him. But turning around and seeing His disciples, He rebuked Peter and *said, 'Get behind Me, Satan; for you are not setting your mind on God's interests, but man's.'"
>
> Mark 8:32

Jesus knew His purpose and destiny. He operated with a clear vision of His mandate and had already pre-determined to accomplish His goal no matter what. When Peter steps in with what could be perceived as a 'good' motivation to stop his Lord from submitting to death, Jesus brings swift correction. He refers to Peter as 'Satan,' which can also be translated as adversary in this encounter. He corrects Peter in front of the other disciples for having the mindset of man. Peter most likely held the common belief that the Messiah would establish an earthly Kingdom and must not die. They were clueless about how God's plan had to unfold. Jesus brings swift and strong correction in the form of a rebuke.

COACHING

GOOD OR GOD?

By studying this interaction of Jesus rebuking Peter, we learn the seriousness and error of man's natural thinking. Peter is acting in a way that seems right to him. When Jesus states to Peter that he is acting in man's interests, we see that the mind of man is in opposition to the mind of God. We as men can get caught up in planning and masterminding our lives, business endeavors, career paths and many other things, to the point of thinking we have it all figured out. This is most often not the way God will unfold His plan and design for our lives. Peter was most likely masterminding how the Messiah would ascend to the throne in Israel and reorder the political and religious landscape. He may have also been motivated by what his new position would be in this Jesus-led Kingdom, as one who would be part of the inner circle. Jesus fiercely rebukes Peter and his plan.

The keys from this interaction are:

1. Get the mind of God. Seek first the Kingdom and His will before we start envisioning and building our empires.

2. Submit our ways to the Lord. Ask the Lord to search our hearts for hidden motives, and ask Him to replace our ambition with His vision for our lives.

3. Walk with humility, esteeming others in our life higher than ourselves. Stay open to correction and consistently submit our plans to God and others in our lives for godly wisdom.

"And Jesus knowing their thoughts said, 'Why are you thinking evil in your hearts?'"

Matthew 9:4

JESUS IS DISCERNING OF MAN

As Jesus appears on the scene as the miracle worker, word of His fame starts to spread, the crowds are attracted and there is a buzz about the healer who travels from town to town. People come out in droves to see for themselves and get a glimpse of this Galilean preacher. After He performed His first miracle, the number of people following Him exploded.

> "While Jesus was at the Passover Feast, the number of his followers began to grow, and many gave their allegiance to him because of all the miraculous signs they had seen him doing! But Jesus did not yet entrust himself to them, because he knew how fickle human hearts can be. He didn't need anyone to tell him about human nature, for he fully understood what man was capable of doing."
> John 2:23-25 (TPT)

Jesus is consumed with love for us. He wholeheartedly embraces His mission to minister to humanity and walk among the crowds as the Son of Man. He sees human nature first hand and up close, He observed the frenzy of the surrounding crowds as they all press in to see or experience the next miracle. They celebrate and cheer Him on as He confronts the Pharisees. They look on in astonishment as people are delivered from demons and they are amazed when they witness the supernatural power He demonstrates. Despite all this, Jesus didn't place His trust in the fickle crowds that celebrated the works He was doing in that moment. He understands the fallen human condition.

Although He is driven with an intense love for us, He did not place His trust in men. He knows they are doubleminded, unstable and can lack character.

JESUS LOVES THE SINNER AND DOES NOT ACCEPT THE SIN

Jesus demonstrates that we can unconditionally love someone and still not accept the sin in their life. Jesus, the one who knew no sin, loves the sinner with an all-consuming love, a love so powerful that it brings Him to the cross. Yet despite loving us, He hates the sin and the destructive effect it has in our lives. Everywhere He goes He reverses the effect of sin, bringing healing, deliverance, forgiveness and restoration. He never sympathizes with or embraces our fallen human condition. He demonstrates empathy that inspires action.

> **Jesus demonstrates empathy that inspires action**

When people come in contact with Jesus, He relates to them with understanding that draws them towards Him without condoning or accepting the sin in their lives. Those who respond to this approach are inspired to leave their sin behind and follow Jesus.

JESUS DOES NOT PUT HIS TRUST IN MAN

> "But Jesus would not entrust himself to them, because he knew all people."
>
> John 2:24 (NET)

Jesus did not rely on those around Him. His mission would not succeed or fail based on the actions or inaction of those closest to Him. His mission was built on reliance upon His Father. In the Garden of Gethsemane, the disciples scattered the moment confrontation came. Jesus was unmoved by their decision because He understands the frail nature of man.

You cannot earn the Love of God; it is a free gift offered to all. However, trust is different. There is no performance or works that you can offer to earn more of God's love for you. It is unconditional and unwarranted. Despite loving us, Jesus does not trust man. He shows us it is possible to love someone and still have discernment, not fully entrusting or relying on them.

TRUST IS EARNED NOT GIVEN

We see in the Kingdom that trust is earned. We are called to be discerning. When Jesus sends out His followers to minister, He tells them to be wise as serpents and harmless as doves. Exercising discernment is not a weapon, rather, it offers us protection. Trust is earned, not given. In the Parables of the Talents and the Minas, we see Jesus illustrate testing by allowing the servants who were provided money to invest freely to prove themselves. Those proven to be good stewards received more resources and authority. They earned trust with the master and were promoted accordingly.

COACHING

As men we are called to love others and walk in mercy. We are the leaders of our families and we need to exercise discernment in all areas and relationships to create a safe environment for those around us. We are not to inherently trust anyone who comes across our path, even those who claim to be Christians. Discernment does not mean that we treat everyone with suspicion, but rather we take our time as we form our opinions of others based on observable behaviors and the leading of the Holy Spirit within us.

THE STANDARD IS HIGHER FOR LEADERS

When Paul lists the qualifications of those who would be appointed to leadership positions within the church, he provides qualities that those around them would be able to observe and test through the relationship. These are found in 1 Timothy 3:1-7. We started this chapter with Jesus as our model for not placing immediate trust in others, but rather using wisdom and discernment. I would like to close this chapter by asking us to look in the mirror and uncover what's in our heart. For those of us aspiring to leadership and positions of influence, in what ways has God tested us in our preparation and how are we doing?

Some practical areas we need to exercise discernment are:

- In our relationships
- In our business
- With our family
- Before major decisions are made

COACHING

I have found that God sharpens our discernment through some of the following ways:

- The written Word of God
- The voice of the Holy Spirit
- Through the wisdom of a counselor
- Through our internal convictions
- Through an inner peace

"Then his disciples approached him and said, "Don't you know that what you just said offended the Pharisees?"

Matthew 15:12 (TPT)

JESUS IS NOT SAFE

JESUS BREAKS RELIGIOUS TRADITIONS

Jesus was viewed as a revolutionary among the religious scribes and Pharisees. They viewed Him as someone subversive; someone seeking to destroy the forms and rituals they held dear. As the promised Messiah, Jesus doesn't conform to the traditional view held in Israel at the time of His appearing. He didn't look or act like the Messiah they were looking for. Instead, Jesus labels Himself as the 'Son of Man' and identifies with His humanity as He uproots the traditions of ancient Israel.

Jesus is not religious. He is seen defying the religious traditions of the Jewish faith as He fulfills the law and prepares the people for a new covenant God will make with man. Consider the new paradigm Jesus presents as He departs from long-held ideas of what is proper.

- Forgives sins
- Eats with sinners
- Elevates women
- Heals on the Sabbath
- Openly condemns the Pharisees' use of 'corban'
- Defends His disciples when they don't ceremonially wash their hands
- He allows His disciples to pluck grain on the Sabbath
- He points out the flaws with the religious leaders – their outward keeping of the commandments, but wrong inner attitudes
- Responds to religious accusations with a question, and then illustrates their hypocrisy
- Exposes the religious leaders in public, among the gaze of the crowds, in a direct confrontation

Mark chapter 7 contains the account of the religious scholars questioning Jesus in attempt to correct His disciples. They neglect to eat without first going through the ceremonial washings and traditions of the elders. Jesus exposes their hypocrisy in requiring so much in the way of keeping man-made traditions and departing from the heart of God's law. He ends this confrontation with explaining to the crowd what truly corrupts.

> "Then Jesus called the crowd together again, saying, 'Hear my words, all of you, and take them to heart. What truly contaminates a person is not what he puts into his body, but what comes out. That's what makes a person defiled.'"
>
> Mark 7:14 (TPT)

Jesus changes and challenges the organizational structure. This is the pattern he demonstrates:

COACHING

It is very easy for us to develop traditions and rituals that become our normal operating system out of repetition and habit. Many times it is our mundane routines and mindless activities that hold us back from our breakthrough. The 'religious' attitude Jesus confronts in ancient Israel is their outward form of what is proper while they disregarded the spirit of the law.

As men we must constantly be aware of going through the motions. We tend to get locked in routines that keep us trapped and don't allow us to breakthrough to the next level in our relationships and in life. Most men are fathering based on outdated traditions they observed through society or the one they were modeled from their father.

We also can get mundane with how we steward our relationships with our wives. It is very easy to fall into the trap of a vicious cycle, where the same behavior patterns occur and are never confronted, challenged, broken and rebuilt. Our self-limiting habits are not limited to our relationships only. They can show up in every area of life, from our morning routine, to the ritual we walk through as soon as we walk through the door after work. Jesus is not safe in the way He addresses habits that need to be changed and priorities that to be aligned. Take an inventory of the routines in your life and relationships that may have become 'status quo'. Identify the cycles and patterns that need to be confronted and changed.

"Upon entering Jerusalem Jesus went directly into the temple area and drove away all the merchants who were buying and selling their goods. He overturned the tables of the money changers and the stands of those selling doves. And he said to them, 'My dwelling place will be known as a house of prayer, but you have made it into a hangout for thieves!'"

Matthew 21:12-13 (TPT)

JESUS IS A MAN OF PURPOSE AND PASSION

In the opening verse of this chapter we find the account of Jesus moving with mission directly into the temple which has been transformed into a marketplace (Matt 21:12-13). He flips tables and clears out the courts of commerce. He was making a way for the downtrodden of His day. The bazaar that the merchants set up blocked many from drawing close to the sanctuary within the temple.

Following this demonstration of strength by Jesus in Matthews account, the scene shifts. Children gather around Jesus, and then comes another interaction between Jesus and the Pharisees.

By clearing out the merchants, Jesus was instituting order. The broken can now draw close to Him, and the children can come to adore Him. The religious elite are once again outraged. Jesus gracefully moves from righteous anger to a gentle, healing touch and playful children singing His praise, to correction of the Pharisees. See all of these acts together as compassion. To demonstrate righteous anger and the destruction of these corrupt practices is motivated by compassion. The entrance to the sanctuary had to be opened for healing. Prior to this, even priests who were lame were not allowed to enter the sanctuary. Jesus' invitation for healing in this location breaks the traditions and offends the religious.

Picture the scene: Jesus arrives on a donkey and the city is shaking in an uproar as He dismounts the animal. He walks with single-eye purpose and intention as He goes directly into the temple area to confront and make an open spectacle of those merchants conducting commerce within the sacred area of the temple.

Jesus did not hide His emotion. You can see the sweat on His brow from the Middle-Eastern sun, as He cuts through the crowds to bring a confrontation. Jesus spent the majority of His earthly life as a builder, so we know He was not a weak man. He calls upon this physical strength as He flips tables, rebukes merchants and tears down their display's, all in the presence of dazed onlookers and a stunned religious order. Jesus is not weak; Jesus is not safe. Jesus brings disruption where things are out of order. He tears down and breaks up, then He rebuilds, aligns and constructs according to the proper order of His Kingdom.

He never claimed to bring peace. He wields a sword; His words and actions cut and scar the religious and political order He confronts. He separates families and brings everyone He comes in contact with to a decision. You cannot call Him good and not accept Him. You cannot remain lukewarm or neutral in your feelings towards Him. There is a fire in His eyes; an unshakable, unforgettable fire. When you see it, you will forever be changed once your eyes lock on His. Yes, He brings you to a decision. It is either accept Him and follow Him, or reject Him and turn your back. There is no fence to straddle, line to walk or boundary to flirt with. If it is not an all-out embrace of all that He is, then it is rejection of Jesus Himself and all He offers you.

When you say yes, prepare for a new way of living and learning. He is a gentle, compassionate Shepherd, a loving Father and friend. He is also a master Teacher who brings you into truth and leads you into places that may leave you questioning if He is still with you. His ways are not our ways. He sees situations differently than you and I, because He has a view of the entire chessboard. Enrollment in His school, the school of His Spirit, has no time limits. He will test you…and the good news is that if you reject or fail the test, you will get to take it over. He will break you, so that you can be used. He does not need your natural talents, skills and abilities. He wants your total trust, strength and faith to be found in Him and not in yourself.

He does not build on the faulty foundations of man. He will clear the ground and level the field to start over again if necessary. He is the Chief Cornerstone, building everything He constructs on an immovable foundation with symmetry and precise measurement. His building materials are not of this world. If you are attempting to build your own life without Him, you are at best using wood, hay and stubble. Your resources will be found lacking on the day He tests all things by fire (Psalm 18:8). Many good, tall and seemingly strong structures will topple on that day. Even monuments and buildings with His name on them, and even those that were built by those who requested His blessing.

He is returning for a mature body of believers that is without a stain or wrinkle; a church that has placed their trust and found their strength in Him alone. These are the co-laborers, the partners, the wise builders who built with un-earthly resources, spiritual stones, gems, gold and spiritual substance that is not of this world.

This is what we are pursuing, He is not merely our mentor, teacher, friend or role model. Life with Him is an all-consuming fire and passion. It is His life within us, pulsating and beating with the heartbeat of Heaven. It consumes and envelopes, stretching the internal boundary where soul meets spirit.

The two-edged sword that proceeds out of His mouth is for us. It is to separate your soul and that which is within your humanistic, logical and emotional realm from the realm of the Spirit. He discerns your innermost aspirations, selfish ambition and roots of pride to lay them bare and expose them in the light.

He is coming for everything.
He wants it all.

Book VI: Love

THE CROSS

THE WORK OF THE CROSS

———

THE WAY OF THE CROSS

———

THE CALL

"Greater love has no one than this, that one lay down his life for his friends."

John 15:13

THE WORK OF THE CROSS

We have examined the life of Jesus in His humanity and the standard He sets for us as men through what He models, His methods and His actions. We have focused on a few of His characteristics and there are many more to be discovered (not only as a Man but preeminently as we set out to meet Him as Son of God). All of His characteristics can be summed up in His character which is undeniably His love.

This one word 'love,' is the total sum of all that we observe through the entire word of God and His eternal purpose from before the foundation of the world. "For God so loved the world that He gave us His Son..." It was the ultimate love of the Father to give us the Son; it is the unwavering Love for His Father and for you and me that drives Jesus to empty Himself in the ultimate expression of humility: submitting Himself to the brutal atrocity of the cross.

We cannot begin to fathom the amount of love that commits Jesus to bow before rough Roman centurions as they beat Him with their hardened fists, rods and leather whips embedded with fragments of bone and glass. See Jesus who was mercilessly marred and unrecognizable from the brutal beating at the hands of these barbarians, then forced to carry the instrument of His death up a hill known as the place of the skull.

With His beaten body pulsating with pain from the riveting torture, mockery and humiliation of the last 24 hours of His earthly life, He now makes His way to the pinnacle of the work He must accomplish for humanity. It is love that consumes Him as He takes each step and maintains His focus. In each breath that He inhales, He is obsessed by an overwhelming love for you.

This is the character of Jesus

LOVE

Selfless, limitless and undeniable…

…all for you and for me.

The work of the cross pays a price that we could never pay to bring us into a new position. When Jesus declared,

He was declaring the finished and fulfilled work of our salvation. He purchased our salvation and way back to the Father through what He accomplished on the cross. The ransom has been paid, the gift has been purchased and it is His will that none will perish; that all will choose to receive Him as Savior and Lord.

THE WAY OF THE CROSS

Making the decision to become a disciple and follow Jesus does not come with the promise of a challenge-free life. Jesus once told His disciples that a disciple is not above his teacher (Matthew 10:24). For the disciple there is a cost just as there was for the teacher. The invitation to "follow Me" cannot be divorced from self-denial and the cross.

> "Then Jesus said to His disciples, 'If anyone wishes to come after Me, he must deny himself, and take up his cross and follow Me.'"
> Matthew 16:24

The finished work of the cross opens the door to salvation and relationship with Jesus. You are called to be His disciple and walk the same road as Him. The way of the cross is the path we are called to walk as we follow the Savior and our risen Lord to higher ground. In God's Kingdom, the way down is up. This means as we walk the way of the cross we will be elevated.

> **As we pick up our cross, Jesus gains more ground within us and we gain more ground in our life**

His call for us is to come up higher. Throughout His earthly life we see many experiences of Jesus on mountains. These are literal and symbolic mountains as we discover He calls us to climb the mountains, take the high ground and elevate our perspective in all areas.

- After His temptation in the wilderness, Jesus ends His 40 day fast on a mountain (Matthew 4:8).
- Jesus delivers what has been called the constitution of Heaven's Kingdom on a mountainside. This is also commonly known as the 'sermon on the mount' (Matthew 5).

- On more than one occasion we find Jesus going up mountains to pray (Matthew 14:23, Mark 6:46, Luke 6:12, John 6:15).
- We find Him ministering and healing the sick from a mountain (Matthew 15:29-31).
- His transfiguration occurred on a mountain (Matthew 17:1).
- His final discourse is given from a mountain (Matthew 24:3).
- His commissioning of the apostles happens on top of a mountain (Matthew 28:16-20).

As we pick up our cross, Jesus gains more ground within us and we gain more ground in our life. The earthly mission of Jesus was not complete with the cross or the grave. The ultimate finish was His ascent, His going up, and if you are to follow in His way, that is your destiny as well.

"FOLLOW ME"

-Jesus

THE CALL

Men, Jesus is calling you

The invitation of Jesus to "follow Me" demands a response. He is more than a good role-model, a wise teacher or another 'prophet.' If you only see Him as a model for self-discipline, an ancient teacher of self-help or a philosopher on the law of attraction, you have missed the opportunity and the invitation He offers you.

Have you been living only for yourself?
Are you distant in your walk with Jesus?
Do you know Him?

If you can acknowledge that there is more…

More that Jesus has for you in life,
More that is required of you,
More that you can receive from Him,
More power available to you…
To become who you were designed to be,

And if this has been missing…

Then today is the day to re-pledge your life to Him and His Kingdom.

If you do not know Jesus, He invites you to meet Him today. We are all born sinners in need of a Savior. We must meet Him as Lord and Savior to receive a new, sinless nature as He fills us with His Spirit and imparts His life within us. Transforming us into a new creation, He makes us a new man.

If you would like to respond to His call, change your direction and take the first step along the path that has been presented within these pages, pray the following and align your heart, will and actions with this declaration:

Lord Jesus, I come before You today as a sinner in need of a Savior. I repent of my sins and ask You to forgive me. I receive You as My Lord and Savior and invite You into my life. I pledge my allegiance to You this day. I lay down the old things in my life and choose to follow You. Fill me with Your Holy Spirit and teach me Your ways as I seek to follow You.

THE MAN WHO WROTE THE BOOK

Josh Khachadourian is a husband, father, leader and coach on a mission to lift up Jesus as the Standard by which all of life's decisions, passions and pursuits will be measured by.

"The Standard is not about me, it's about showing men the way to true manhood and masculinity, the way God designed us. Jesus sets the Standard, He not only shows us the way, He is the way."

Founded on a scripture in Isaiah 59, Josh has created Standard 59 as an answer to mediocrity and a call to ascend in all areas of life. You can learn more by visiting www.standard59.com

BOOK JOSH TO SPEAK AT YOUR NEXT EVENT

Josh speaks and trains on a variety of topics. Inquire about speaking and podcast interviews by emailing: Josh@standard59.com

FREE GIFT

GET THE MAP

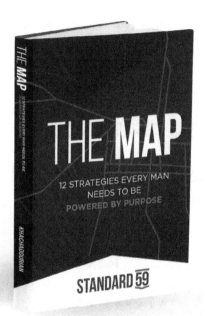

https://www.standard59.com/THEMAP

12 STRATEGIES EVERY MAN NEEDS TO BE POWERED BY PURPOSE

ARE YOU READY TO TAKE DOMINION IN LIFE WITH JESUS AS THE STANDARD?

Listen to the Raising The Standard Podcast to Get Weekly Motivation for the Kingdom Driven Man

- LEVEL UP IN LIFE WITH A BLUEPRINT FOR YOU AS A KINGDOM MAN
- STEP INTO BIBLICAL MASCULINITY WITH THE RIGHT DAILY ACTIONS
- GET STRATEGIES AND TACTICS ON HOW TO EXPAND THE KINGDOM OF GOD IN YOUR LIFE TODAY

RAISING THE STANDARD

LEADERSHIP, MINDSET AND DEVELOPMENT FOR THE KINGDOM MAN

Listen Today on Your Favorite Podcast Platform

INTRODUCE MEN TO THE STANDARD

By leaving a review on Amazon you help Men Discover Jesus as
THE STANDARD

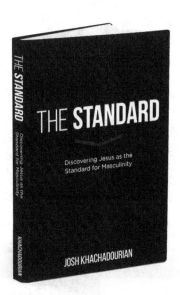

SCAN THIS CODE WITH YOUR CAMERA TO
LEAVE A REVIEW OR VISIT:

https://amzn.to/31pH2di

TAKE THE KINGDOM DRIVEN MAN CHALLENGE

SPIRITUAL FITNESS MEETS PHYSICAL FITNESS

The Kingdom Driven Man Challenge is a 40 day Spiritual, Physical and Mindset Transformation Program. Over the course of 6 weeks You will be Equipped with Daily Spiritual Missions built to Empower You to take the territory God has for You.

☑ **ACCESS YOUR UNFAIR ADVANTAGE**
Through a New Spiritual Morning Routine

☑ **MASTER DAILY DISCIPLINE**
With the Kingdom Athlete Workouts

☑ **UPGRADE YOUR ENVIRONMENT**
In an Elite Brotherhood with Your Vision, Mission and Values

SIGN UP TODAY AT KingdomDrivenMan.com

Made in the USA
Middletown, DE
29 March 2022